B 52540 8

FAIRCHILD

HISTORY
OF THE
NEW YORK
ACADEMY
OF
SCIENCES

Q
11
v53
F3

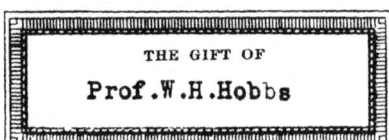

Q
11
.N538
F3

Wm H Hobbs

Q
11
.N538
F3

Presented by H L Fairchild
Sept. 22nd, 1893.

History
of the
New York Academy of Sciences

Five hundred copies printed, of which this is number

.

A History

OF THE

New York Academy of Sciences

FORMERLY THE

Lyceum of Natural History

BY

HERMAN LE ROY FAIRCHILD
Recording Secretary

Read, in abstract, before the Society, May 10, 1886

NEW YORK
PUBLISHED BY THE AUTHOR

M DCCC LXXXVII

Copyright, 1887, by
H. L. FAIRCHILD

GILLISS BROTHERS & TURNURE
THE ART AGE PRESS
400 & 402 WEST 14TH STREET, N. Y.

PREFACE.

THE sketch of the origin and growth of the Lyceum which Dr. John Torrey read at the celebration of the semi-centennial of the Society (see Section IX.), was not preserved. The need, however, of some printed information concerning the history and present condition of the Society had long been recognized, and at the meeting on June 9, 1884, the author presented a motion, which was adopted, authorizing and requesting the Secretary to prepare such a manual. As this work had not been done when the author became Secretary, he undertook, therefore, to gather the desired information.

The intention was to make a paper of such length that it could be printed in an issue of the "Transactions." The sources of information, however, exceeded expectation; the early minutes were found intact, and interesting material so accumulated that the paper outgrew the plan, and it became necessary to publish it separately.

The matter was read at the Academy meeting of May 10, 1886—the fiftieth anniversary of the first meeting held in the Lyceum Building—at which time the first minute-book and records and relics were shown. New material has since been added, and some changes made.

The Secretary was given permission to publish the work upon his own responsibility, the text to be subject to the approval of the Council. The matter has received such approval, and is now placed before the members and friends of the Society.

The delay in publishing has made it possible to incorparate several recent changes in the By-Laws, and to bring the descriptive matter up to date.

Especial thanks are due to Mr. J. H. Redfield, for his generous contribution relating to a most interesting epoch in the life of the Society—the time of the Lyceum Building and that immediately following. This matter will be found in quotation marks and designated ($_R$), where not directly credited. To Dr. Charles E. West and to many other friends the author is gratefully indebted.

New York, February, 1887.

TABLE OF CONTENTS.

SECTION I.
ORIGIN, ORGANIZATION AND INCORPORATION, . . PAGE 1

SECTION II.
ORIGINAL MEMBERS, ... 21

SECTION III.
PLACES OF MEETING, AND THE LYCEUM BUILDING, . 28

SECTION IV.
OFFICERS OF THE SOCIETY, 1817 TO 1887, . . . 52

SECTION V.
BIOGRAPHICAL SKETCHES, ... 57

SECTION VI.
COLLECTIONS, ... 97

SECTION VII.
LIBRARY, ... 108

SECTION VIII.
PUBLICATIONS, ... 118

Section IX.
Semi-Centennial Celebration, ... 124

Section X.
Change of Name and Constitution, ... 126

Section XI.
Membership, ... 132

Section XII.
Charter, Order of Court, Constitution and By-Laws, ... 163

Index of Persons, ... 183
General Index, ... 187

ILLUSTRATIONS.

Portraits.

JOHN S. NEWBERRY,	Frontispiece
	FACING PAGE
JOHN B. BECK,	8
JAMES E. DE KAY,	16
CHARLES A. JOY,	20
SAMUEL L. MITCHILL,	56
JOSEPH DELAFIELD,	64
JOHN TORREY,	68
WILLIAM COOPER,	72
ROBERT H. BROWNNE,	76
WILLIAM C. REDFIELD,	80
BENJAMIN N. MARTIN,	84
ASA GRAY,	88
CHARLES M. WHEATLEY,	92
THOMAS BLAND,	96
JOHN C. JAY,	100
JOHN H. REDFIELD,	104
ROBERT DINWIDDIE,	108
THOMAS EGLESTON,	112
ALEXIS A. JULIEN,	116
JOHN H. HINTON,	120
H. CARRINGTON BOLTON,	124
ALBERT R. LEEDS,	128
DANIEL S. MARTIN,	132
OLIVER P. HUBBARD,	144

Illustrations

Portraits.—Continued.

	FACING PAGE
LOUIS ELSBERG,	152
WILLIAM P. TROWBRIDGE,	160
HERMAN L. FAIRCHILD,	168

Buildings.

COLLEGE OF PHYSICIANS AND SURGEONS IN BARCLAY ST.,	28
NEW YORK INSTITUTION,	32
NEW YORK DISPENSARY,	36
THE LYCEUM BUILDING,	40
STUYVESANT INSTITUTE,	44
UNIVERSITY MEDICAL COLLEGE IN 14TH ST	48
HAMILTON HALL, COLUMBIA COLLEGE,	50

SECTION I.

Origin, Organization and Incorporation.

S the LYCEUM OF NATURAL HISTORY, and under its present name, the NEW YORK ACADEMY OF SCIENCES has an honorable record of nearly three-fourths of a century. Organized February 24, 1817, the Society was chartered April 20, 1818, and was re-named in 1876. In comparison with existing American Scientific Societies it ranks fourth in point of age. The American Philosophical Society, of Philadelphia, dates from 1769; the American Academy of Arts and Sciences, in Boston, began in 1780; and the Academy of Natural Sciences, of Philadelphia, in 1812. The latter was not incorporated until 1817.

To the degree that any one society can, in a great city, be a scientific centre, the Lyceum and Academy has been that centre in New York. Its resident membership has included the great majority of men who, in and about the city, have been identified with scientific work; while the roll of Honorary, Corresponding and Resident Members might well be taken as the list of those eminent men whose labors have made the nineteenth century the most remarkable for scientific and material progress in the world's history.

The origin and early history of the Society are not left in obscurity; but our knowledge is chiefly derived from the records of meetings. Unwisely, no history was written and preserved while men were living who participated in the formation of the Society, or who knew the facts. Fortunately, however, the early minutes are preserved. With the Library, these records have escaped the catastrophes which destroyed the collections.

The story of the birth and early days in the life of the Society can not be better told than by quoting in full the earliest record. With some slight changes in punctuation, etc., the following is the writing:

("MINUTES OF THE PROCEEDINGS OF THE LYCEUM OF NATURAL HISTORY, NEW YORK, 1817.")

"At a meeting of a number of Gentlemen favourable to the cultivation of *Natural Science*, held on Wednesday, the 29th January, 1817, at the Hall of the College of Physicians and Surgeons, in Barclay Street, New York, Doctor Samuel L. Mitchell was called to the chair, and Frederick C. Schaeffer appointed Secretary.

"The object was stated to be the consideration and adoption of measures for instituting a *Cabinet of Natural History*, in this city. After some discussion, Dr. A. W. Ives, Revd. F. C. Schaeffer and Dr. P. S. Townsend were appointed a Committee to report on the subject, to the meeting at some future day.—Adjourned.

"Signed,   F. C. SCHAEFFER,
                              Secy."

"MONDAY, February 3, 1817.

"The Gentlemen present at a former meeting being again convened, the Committee appointed for the purpose made the following *Report :*

"That they have taken into consideration the subject of a proposed establishment in this city for the cultivation of Natural Science, and from the various and ample information presented to them, do not hesitate in declaring such an Institution in their opinion perfectly practicable.

"The Committee feel unauthorized to enter into detail at this meeting, lest it be deemed premature or proceeding beyond the limits assigned to them at the last meeting. They, therefore, on the present occasion take the liberty to recommend that the Gentlemen present, favourable to such an Institution, meet at this place on Friday noon, Feby. 7, 1817, and that they be requested to invite such of their friends as would probably unite with them in the accomplishment of the object proposed.

"Signed,   A. W. IVES,
           F. C. SCHAEFFER,
           P. S. TOWNSEND,
                        Committee."

"The Report was adopted and the recommendation agreed to in the form of a Resolution; after which the meeting adjourned to the 7th of February."

"NEW YORK, Feby. 7, 1817.

"The Association convened pursuant to adjournment, when Doctor Mitchell took the chair and Dr. Eddy was appointed Secretary.

"The Minutes of the preceding meetings were read and approved, and in conformity with the report of the committee as contained in the Minutes of the last meeting—it was Resolved, that a Committee of three be appointed to propose a form of Constitution for the organization of this Association—and to report thereon at the next meeting. Mr. Henry Dodge, Dr. C. W. Eddy and Mr. Rafinesque were selected for that purpose, and as it was deemed necessary that early steps be taken to procure rooms where the Association might at all times be convened, and to deposit such objects in *Natural History* as should be judged worthy of preservation, it was, on motion, Resolved, that a Committee of three, (of which the chairman of this meeting be one) be appointed to obtain such accommodation. Doctors Townsend and Bliss were adjoined to the Chairman, Dr. Mitchell, to carry that resolution into effect.—Adjourned to meet at College Hall, on Thursday next, the 13th inst., at noon.

"Signed, CASPAR WISTAR EDDY,

Secy."

"NEW YORK, Feby. 13, 1817.

"The Association met pursuant to adjournment—Dr. Mitchell in the chair and Dr. Eddy, Secretary—Minutes of the preceding meeting read and approved. The Committee appointed to draft a Constitution, submitted a form of Constitution for the consideration of the Association, when, after some discussion, the first, second and third articles were adopted—the fourth, after some amendment, was also adopted. The Committee to obtain rooms reported progress and were continued in their duty. The Society adjourned till tomorrow, at 12 o'clock, at the College Hall.

"Signed, C. W. EDDY,

Secy."

"NEW YORK, Feby. 14, 1817.

"Society met agreeably to adjournment. Dr. Mitchell in the chair. Dr. Eddy, Secy. After some discussion several more articles were adopted, with amendments, when they again adjourned to the 15th Feby., at noon.

"Signed, C. W. EDDY,

Secy."

Origin and Early Days

"NEW YORK, Feby. 15, 1817.

" Society again met. Dr. Benjamin P. Kissam in the chair and Dr. Eddy, Secy., the constitution still under consideration, and, after many amendments, the Society adjourned to meet on the 17th, at noon.

"Signed,   C. W. EDDY, Secy."

"NEW YORK, Feby. 17, 1817.

" Dr. Kissam in the Chair and Dr. Eddy, Secy. After some further amendments to the Constitution, adjourned till tomorrow.

"Signed,   C. W. EDDY, Secy."

"NEW YORK, Feby. 18, 1817.

" Meeting held pursuant to adjournment. Dr. Kissam in the chair and Dr. Eddy, Secy. After some further amendments, the Constitution was taken as amended and passed, and ordered to be engrossed by the Committee who drew it up, when the Society adjourned to meet at Harmony Hall to make choice of officers for the ensuing year.

"Signed,   CASPAR WISTAR EDDY, Secy."

"NEW YORK, Feby. 24, 1817.

" The *Lyceum of Natural History* met according to adjournment at Harmony Hall, at 7 o'clock, P. M. Dr. Mitchell was called to the chair. On motion, made and carried, a committee of three was appointed to superintend the signing of the Constitution, and the election of officers for the ensuing year. Dr. Eddy, Revd. F. C. Schaeffer and John B. Beck were selected for that purpose. The following gentlemen then affixed their names to the Constitution, viz. :

Samuel L. Mitchell,	D'Jurco Knevels,
Caspar Wistar Eddy,	John Torrey,
John B. Beck,	Wm. Cooper,
F. C. Schaeffer,	Thos. Eddy, Junr.,
Benj. P. Kissam,	B. R. Greenland,
Ezekiel R. Baudoine.	M. D. L. F. Erving,
Francis Morton,	Lewis C. Beck,
D. L. M. Peixotto,	Charles C. Townsend,
John W. Francis,	J. Roane,
Henry M. Francis,	R. B. Owen,

Cornelius P. Heermans.

"The Lyceum next proceeded to the choice of Officers, when the following Gentlemen were declared duly elected, viz.:

SAMUEL L. MITCHELL, M. D., &c., President.
CASPAR WISTAR EDDY, M. D., First Vice-President.
REVD. F. C. SCHAEFFER, Second Vice-President.
JOHN W. FRANCIS, M. D., &c., Corresponding Secy.
JOHN B. BECK, A. M., Recording Secy.
BENJAMIN P. KISSAM, M. D., Treasurer.
JOHN TORREY,
D'JURCO V. KNEVELS,   Curators.
EZEKIEL R. BAUDOINE, A. B.,

"A Committee composed of John B. Beck, Revd. F. C. Schaeffer, Dr. Kissam, Dr. Eddy and Dr. Francis was appointed to draw up certain bye-laws for the better regulation of the Association. On motion, adjourned to meet on the following Monday at the College Physicians and Surgeons, Barclay street, at four o'clock P. M.

"JOHN B. BECK,
Secy."

The name LYCEUM first appears in the minutes of this meeting of organization, the first "*Annual Meeting.*" (See Section VI.)

In a biographical sketch of Dr. Torrey (Bulletin Torrey Botanical Club, IV., 30) Dr. Thurber says that "the incorporators met to adopt their charter in one

Origin and Early Days 7

of the rooms of the College of Physicians and Surgeons in Barclay street. Upon the adoption of the charter they adjourned to a well-known public house and celebrated the event in mugs of ale, paid for by a general contribution of pennies." He certainly had in mind the occasion of the adoption of the constitution as recorded above; for the adoption of the charter occurred more than a year later, and in the rooms of the Society in the New York Institution. But concerning the festivity he is doubtless right, for Dr. Torrey is reported as saying at the semi-centennial meeting of the Society, that "there was no grand banquet—only crackers and cheese and a gallon of good beer." It should be observed, however, that this particular meeting was not held in the college, as were all the others, but in the "well-known public house" (see page 28) where the mild celebration took place. The latter was but natural, considering the place and circumstances, the habits of the time and the youthfulness of the members.

All of these early minutes, and those of the year following, are apparently in the handwriting of John B. Beck, the first elected Recording Secretary. He doubtless copied from the manuscript records of the previously appointed secretaries. The writing was done after March 17th. The orthography of the President's name is incorrect in these minutes.

The newspapers of that time make no mention of these meetings as a matter of news. The only reference found is a "communication" in the *Commercial Advertiser* of February 27, 1817, which was evidently sent by some member of the new Society, stating that the Society had been organized, and giving a list of its officers and briefly describing its purpose.

The record of the next meeting, March 3, 1817, states that Drs. Townsend (probably Dr. P. S. Townsend) and Aydelott appeared and signed the constitution ; and that a cordial letter was read from John W. Francis, declining the office of Corresponding Secretary.

"Dr. Mitchell, as President, then delivered an interesting address on the subjects in Zoölogy which particularly called for the attention and investigation of the members. On motion of Dr. Francis, the thanks of the Lyceum were unanimously returned to the President for his able communication."

This inaugural address by the President was, apparently, the first scientific matter presented to the Society.

The record further states that J. Clements, veterinary surgeon, and Stephen A. Rich were proposed as Resident Members by Dr. Eddy.

Following these proposals, a committee was "appointed to consider what persons were entitled to be considered as Original Members of this association, besides those who had signed the Constitution at the first regular meeting."

At this meeting occurred, also, the first appropriation of money: " one Dollar for the use of a room at Harmony Hall," and " one Dollar for a blank book containing the Constitution" of the Lyceum.

At the meeting of March 10, 1817, Dr. Eddy was in the chair, and eleven other persons were present. John Le Conte, Esq., was elected to fill the vacancy in the office of Corresponding Secretary. This seems irregu-

John B. Beck Recg. Secy

lar, as his name does not occur in the list of signers of the constitution. It appears, however, in the printed list of members.

Mr. J. Clements was elected a Resident Member, being the first person to receive that honor in regular form.

The Committee on Original Membership made their report. (For this report see page 21.)

At this meeting the "Bye-Laws" were reported and adopted. A committee was appointed to prepare an article to give publicity to the Society. Dr. Eddy gave notice that as soon as a place was prepared he should deposit a list of books, which list is written in full in the minutes. But the titles of these books are not in the printed catalogues of the Library.

On March 17th Rev. F. C. Schaeffer occupied the chair, and seven other persons were present. The election of Corresponding and Honorary Members was indefinitely deferred. There were several nominations awaiting action; and perhaps they were not all satisfactory. The membership of the Society was always carefully guarded. The first election to honorary membership took place April 21, 1817.

A committee was appointed at this meeting to report upon lectures on Natural History subjects, by the members at each session.

The Treasurer was directed to pay $3.50 for a Minute Book. Probably the one which contains these minutes is the particular book.

At the next meeting, March 24th, thirteen persons were present, with Dr. Eddy in the chair. Dr. B. Kissam was formally thanked for a ballot box which he presented to the Society. The action of March 10th relating to the publication of a notice of the Society was rescinded, and a new committee " was appointed to prepare a Circular for publication."

"Mr. Rafinesque, from the Committee appointed to examine certain Cabinets offered for sale," reported adversely, on account of the cost. The Committee was continued. (See Section VI.)

The Committee on Lectures appointed at the preceding meeting made their report, which is worth quoting in full. This report is printed along with the first list of members, and there differs slightly from the record in the minutes. The following is from the printed copy:

"The undersigned * * * * *recommend*,

"1. That every Resident Member shall within six months, and every Corresponding Member within twelve months after his admission, read or cause to be read before the Society a paper on any subject connected with Natural History, which shall be considered as their *admission paper;* and that every such Resident or Corresponding Member be recommended to furnish at least one other paper during the course of each year.

"2. That the subjects embraced within the views of this Society be divided into as many subdivisions as the nature of its branches will admit, in order that different Gentlemen may be appointed to deliver lectures thereon, so that the Lyceum shall have one lecture, on some one or other of the numerous branches comprehended under the term of *Natural History*, at each of its regular meetings; and that the Lecturer shall in no case occupy the attention of the Society more than one hour at a time.

"3. That it be the duty of the Lecturer to give demonstrations on each article presented to the Society, which shall fall within the limits of his lectureship.

"They, therefore, beg leave to submit the following subdivisions; and suggest that the Gentlemen, whose names are placed opposite

Origin and Early Days

to the respective subdivisions, be appointed to discharge the duties appertaining to the second and third sections of this Report:

Mastodology, *Mammalia*,	Mr. Le Conte.*
Ornithology,	Dr. B. P. Kissam.
Erpetology, *Reptilia*,	Mr. Le Conte.*
Ichthyology,	Dr. Mitchill.
Plaxology, *Crustacea*,	Dr. Mitchill.
Entomology,	Mr. Torrey.
Helminthology, *Vermes*,	Mr. Rafinesque.
Apalology, *Molluscæ*,	Dr. Mitchill.
Polypology, *Polypes*,	Mr. Rafinesque.
Botany,	Dr. Eddy.
Geology,	Dr. Mitchill.
Mineralogy,	Rev. Mr. Schaeffer.
Oryctology, *Fossils*,	Dr. Townshend.
Conchology,	Mr. Knevels.
Hydrology and Atmology,	Mr. Rafinesque.
Taxonomy, *Classification*,	Mr. Rafinesque.
Glossology, *Terminology*,	Mr. Le Conte.*
Zoötomy, *Comparative Anatomy*,	Mr. Clements.

"All of which is respectfully submitted, &c., &c.

"Signed,   F. C. SCHAEFFER,
C. W. EDDY,
C. S. RAFINESQUE,
J. CLEMENTS."

---

* Mr. Le Conte has not yet signified his acceptance of these appointments."

The minutes state that "after considerable discussion on the *constitutionality* of the preceding Report it was finally accepted," and at the next meeting Dr. Eddy, the presiding officer, made the appointments recommended by the Committee.

This plan, however fine in theory, endured the test of use just one year.

The first distinctively scientific paper was read by Mr. C. S. Rafinesque, at the meeting of March 31, 1817. The record is: " Mr. Rafinesque then read two interesting papers, *one* on the *Tubipora striatula*, a new species of fossil, found near Glen's Falls, in the State of New York, *another*, on ten undescribed species of the Genus *Aphis*, found by Mr. Rafinesque in the United States."

The abstract of the proceedings published in Mr. Bigelow's Magazine (see page 15), gives the date of this reading as April 9th (which is incorrect), and adds that he presented a specimen of the fossil for the Cabinet. This is the earliest record of presentation of material for the collections.

The following letter from General J. G. Swift was read April 9, 1817:

WASHINGTON, 2d April, 1817.

DEAR SIR:

The room in the New York Institution which the Corporation destined for the use of the U. S. Military Philosophical Society is at the service of the Lyceum of Natural History upon the conditions mentioned in your interesting letter of 29th ult? I wish success to the Lyceum and that it may become a school for those who desire to contemplate the work of a beneficent creator.

Very respectfully yours, &c.,

To CASPAR W. EDDY, M. D., J. G. SWIFT.
  1st Vice-Prest. Lyceum N. H.

Origin and Early Days

On April 21st, "the Society met agreeably to public notice in the New York Institution," and at this meeting General Swift was unanimously elected an Honorary Member, the rules being suspended for that purpose. This was the first election to that office. General Swift was an eminent engineer in the public service. It was he who, in the great fire of 1835, suggested the blowing up of buildings to stay the flames.

At this meeting, April 21st, Doctor Mitchill made "some highly interesting remarks, tending to prove the horse a native of America." We have no knowledge of either his facts or his arguments, but it is curious that his conception should be proven true by the palæontology of recent years.

The minutes from this time forward abound in references to interesting and valuable scientific material. (See Section VI.) We need not fully quote them, but a running mention of a few items of business and of science from the first year's record will be appropriate:

MAY 5, 1817.—Fifteen members present. Dr. Eddy, Mr. Torrey and Mr. Knevels were appointed a committee to prepare a list of the flora of the country within thirty miles of New York. Their report was made December 17, 1817. (See pages 68–9.)

MAY 12TH.—"The members of the Lyceum were then gratified with a taste of the boiled tongue of the Sea Elephant—Phoca elephantina." Sixteen members were present.

MAY 19TH.—A committee reported that the Constitution was printed, and copies were laid on the table.

A form of Certificate of Membership was adopted, and 250 copies ordered to be printed. Sixteen members present.

CONSTITUTION, &c.

At a Meeting of a number of Gentlemen of the City of New-York, on the 28th *February,* 1817, *the following Preamble and Constitution were unanimously adopted:—*

IMPRESSED with the importance of the study of Natural History as connected with the wants, the comforts, and the happiness of mankind, and particularly as it relates to the illustration of the physical character of the country we inhabit, We the subscribers do hereby agree to associate ourselves for the better cultivation and more extensive promotion of the same; and for our regulations as such Society, do adopt the following

CONSTITUTION.

ARTICLE I.

THIS Society shall be styled "THE LYCEUM OF NATURAL HISTORY."

ARTICLE II.

It shall consist of three classes of Members, viz. Resident, Corresponding, and Honorary—Resident Members, such as dwell in the city of New-York and its immediate vicinity; Corresponding, such as reside at a distance from said city, or in other states;

Reduced fac-simile of first page of Constitution.

A copy of this first printed Constitution is preserved, bound, with the first List of Members, and the Report on Lectureships. It includes XXIV. Articles. No By-laws are appended, although such were reported and adopted March 10th. This seems to have been the first matter printed by the Lyceum. The title-page bears the imprint of George Forman, corner of Fulton and Greenwich streets. A fac-simile of the first page of the text is presented herewith. Singularly, this printed copy of the Constitution gives February 28th as the day of its adoption. This is certainly an error, the correct date being February 18th. The formal organization and signing of the engrossed Constitution occurred February 24th.

Several Articles of this long Constitution were subsequently dropped, condensed or transferred in substance to the By-laws ; and in 1821 the Constitution assumed the form, with ten Articles, which it preserved, essentially, until 1876. (See Section X.)

MAY 26TH.—A committee for printing the list of Members and the Lectureships reported progress. And another committee reported progress in the publishing of the Proceedings in Mr. Bigelow's Magazine.

JUNE 2D.—The President presented the Society with the first number of the Journal of the Academy of Natural Sciences, of Philadelphia, and thanks were formally returned to the Secretary of the Academy.

The committee reported the printing of the list of Officers and Members (see page 22) and the Lectureships. And copies of Bigelow's Magazine containing extracts from the proceedings were laid on the table.

This journal was named " The American Monthly Magazine and Critical Review." It was edited by H. Bigelow, and was published for only two years, 1817–1818. The four volumes which it made are in our Library, and contain the earliest published proceedings of the Lyceum. Some of the meetings, and some papers, are given with considerable fullness. The magazine was of a somewhat miscellaneous character, and well reflects the condition and life of New York City at that time. The births, marriages and deaths are given each month.

JUNE 9TH.—A badge of mourning was ordered to be worn for thirty days in honor of the memory of Dr. James S. Watkins. (See page 22.)

JUNE 23D.—Dr. Mitchill stated "that he had taken an opportunity, afforded in the excursion on board the steam frigate to the Narrows, to present the President of the United States the diploma of membership voted to him by the Lyceum as a testimony of their respect, which was received in a manner gratifying to the feelings of the representative of the Society." *

JULY 14TH.—A long report was read concerning publications, and a " Publication Committee " of five was appointed. A change in the Constitution was adopted, making the initiation fee ten dollars for Resident Members, and five dollars for Corresponding Members.

The fees had been five dollars for Resident, and three dollars for Corresponding Members. The member proposing the candidate was answerable for the payment. The dues were two dollars. In 1821 the fee for Corresponding Members was five dollars, and the dues were four dollars. In 1826 foreign correspondents were exempted. Persons proposing new members were still held accountable for the fees. The fee for Corresponding Member had to be paid at the next meeting after the election. How far these require-

---
* Amer. Monthly Mag., Vol. I., p. 288.

Yours affectionately
J E Worsley

ments held in practice we have no means of judging. In 1837 the requirements were the same, excepting that the annual dues were eight dollars.

JULY 21ST.—Dr. S. Akerly was elected to the vacant office of Corresponding Secretary. Mr. Le Conte had, probably, failed to respond.

JULY 28TH.—Thomas Jefferson, Robert Brown, of London, and De Candolle, of Geneva, were elected Honorary Members. Governor De Witt Clinton was voted for, and failed of election. The vote was reconsidered. But another vote showed less than three-fourths of the members voting, and the matter was deferred indefinitely. The record of the proceeding relating to Governor Clinton is canceled or marked over in the minutes, but not sufficiently to make it illegible. There is, however, no subsequent mention of the matter. We should infer that the scientific men of those days were not entirely without political prejudices.

The injustice, if it was such, to Governor Clinton, was righted later, for on December 14, 1818, he was again proposed, and elected at once under a suspension of the rules.

Mr. Baudoine read a paper at this meeting which discussed the question of the earth's axis having once been in a position 45° inclined to the present position.

AUGUST 4TH.—A standing committee on admission to membership was elected.

OCTOBER 6TH.—A letter from William Smith, of Boston, was read relating to the "Great Sea Serpent." And there was exhibited a specimen supposed by the sender to be a part of the covering or integument of that serpent. The President thought it was the skin of *Esox osseus.*

It will be observed that meetings were held all summer; at what hour we do not know. The last hour mentioned was four o'clock P. M., on March 3d. That it was in the afternoon seems probable, from the fact that it was voted late in October to hold the meetings after November 1st at seven o'clock P. M.

DECEMBER 8TH.—The President and Mr. Anthon were made a committee to draft a charter and prepare a memorial to the Legislature. It was also " Moved, that the Treasurer be authorized to purchase for the Society one pair andirons, shovel and tongs and bellows."

DECEMBER 22D.—Dr. Mitchill was elected to deliver an anniversary address.

DECEMBER 29TH.—" On account of the interruption caused by the alarm of fire the Society adjourned."

FEBRUARY 23, 1818, was the anniversary meeting. Eighteen members were present. The officers elected for the second year of the Society were:

President, Dr. MITCHILL.
Vice-Presidents, Dr. EDDY and Mr. SCHAEFFER.
Corresponding Secretary, Mr. PAULDING.
Recording Secretary, Mr. COOPER.
Treasurer, Dr. KISSAM.
Curators, TORREY, CUMBERLAND, KNEVELS;
to whom were afterwards added Pierce and Clements.

This is the list of officers which appears in the Charter, and consequently has been supposed to be the

Origin and Early Days

first list. (See Section XII.) They were the first officers of the *corporate* Society.

The President delivered an extemporaneous anniversary address. The custom of having an anniversary orator, who was elected a year ahead, was retained for many years. A few of these addresses were printed. Among those preserved is one by Peter S. Townsend, delivered in 1820, and another given by James E. De Kay in 1826.

MARCH 30, 1818.—A report of committee was adopted, dividing the Society into four scientific classes, each distinct, with its own by-laws. These classes were to be Zoölogical, Botanical, Geognostical and Collateral.

The former by-laws were debated, some of them abolished, and the *Lectureships* were formally revoked by the President. Thus ended the first experiment in the classification of the Society's work. (See Section X.)

APRIL 27, 1818.—Henry Meigs was formally thanked for procuring from the Legislature the act of incorporation.

MAY 4, 1818.—The President laid before the Lyceum a certified copy of the *Act of Incorporation*, which was unanimously adopted.

The hour of meeting was changed back to four o'clock, P. M. But this lasted only one month, for June 1, 1818, the hour was made seven and one-half o'clock.

SEPTEMBER 21, 1818.—A committee was appointed to consider and report on the best means of increasing the funds of the Society.

In common with the experience of most scientific bodies, the Lyceum always had need of money. At the Annual Meeting of February 22, 1830, this wail was sent up by the Treasurer: " It is, however, deeply to be lamented that the efforts of our institution for the advancement of the Natural Sciences, whose value is at last beginning to be appreciated, should be so much restrained by the inadequacy of our pecuniary resources."

This sentiment, indeed, sounds familiar to the ears of a later generation.

SECTION II.

Original Members.

THE most active men in the organizing of the Lyceum have been named in the record for February 24, 1817, as having signed the Constitution at the meeting of formal organization.

Drs. Townsend and Aydelott signed the Constitution March 3d.

At the meeting of March 10, 1817, the Committee on Original Membership, which was appointed March 3d, reported as follows :

"*Resolved*, That the following Gentlemen, provided they shall have signed the Constitution or have paid the admission fee, within the period of one month from this date be and are hereby deemed *members* of the Lyceum of Natural History.

Dr. D. W. Kissam,	Mr. Rafinesque.
Dr. S. G. Mott,	Mr. H. Dodge,
Dr. J. Dyckman,	Mr. Corning,
Dr. J. B. Stevenson,	Mr. Watkins,
Dr. Loring,	Mr. Allen.
Dr. J. M. Smith,	

"Signed,   CASPAR WISTAR EDDY,
BENJ. P. KISSAM,
PETER V. TOWNSEND,
Committee."

This report was unanimously accepted. It does not follow, however, that all these names are to be added to the list of original members. The subsequent minutes mention only Mr. Corning as signing the Constitution. The first Constitution, with the signatures, is not preserved; and it is evident that the minutes cannot be relied upon to determine accurately the membership. At the meeting of April 28th, a resolution was adopted, that names of those elected who did not sign the Constitution by the second Monday in May, should be erased from the list. To the time for signing, one month, given in the resolution of election, this was an extension of another month. Most of those persons named in this list did not qualify. Only Dyckman, Rafinesque and Corning appear in the printed list of members, to be presently described. Mr. Watkins seems, however, to have been regarded as a member. He died four days after the printed list was presented to the society, and a badge of mourning, in his honor, was adopted. In later lists his name appears. Subsequent records state that by special resolution Dr. B. A. Akerly and John B. Bogart were made original members, but their names are also lacking in the printed list. Mr. H. Bigelow, editor of the American Monthly Magazine, was also elected June 2d, and signed the Constitution, but his name nowhere appears in print.

The following list of original members is a *literatim* copy of the first printed list, which was laid before the society at its meeting of June 2, 1817.

To these names we have appended some brief information concerning the individuals, gleaned from various sources, which will show something of the personal character of the society at its formation:

Resident Members.

SAMUEL L. MITCHILL, M. D.,
> President. Prof. of Natural History in College of Physicians and Surgeons. Age, 53.

CASPAR WISTAR EDDY, M. D.,
> First Vice-President. Class of 1811, College of Physicians and Surgeons. Age, 27. Nephew of Dr. Mitchill. Died at Bloomingdale, N. Y., July 12, 1828.

JOHN B. BECK, M. D.,
> Recording Secretary. A. B., Columbia College, 1813. Class of 1817, College of Physicians and Surgeons. Age, 22. Died April 9, 1851.

REV. FREDERICK C. SCHAEFFER,
> Second Vice-President. Pastor of St. Matthew's Church (Lutheran), in Walker street.

BENJAMIN P. KISSAM, M. D.,
> Treasurer. Surgeon United States Navy, 1813. Class of 1816, College of Physicians and Surgeons. Died October 6, 1828.

EZEKIEL ROBINS BAUDOUINE,
> Curator. Class of 1818, College of Physicians and Surgeons. Lost at sea.

FRANCIS MORTON,
> Graduate of Columbia, 1815.

D. L. M. PEIXOTTO,
> Columbia, 1816. Class 1819, College of Physicians and Surgeons. Age, 19. Died, New York, May 14, 1843.

JOHN W. FRANCIS, M. D.,
> Columbia College, 1809. Professor Materia Medica, College of Physicians and Surgeons, 1813-16; Professor of Institutes of Medicine, 1816-20; Registrar, 1811-26. Age, 28. Died, New York, February 8, 1861.

HENRY M. FRANCIS,
> Graduate of Columbia, 1808.

D'JURCO V. KNEVELS,
> Curator. Class of 1819, College of Physicians and Surgeons.

JOHN TORREY,
> Curator. Class of 1818, College of Physicians and Surgeons. Age, 21. Died, New York, March 10, 1873.

WILLIAM COOPER,
> Age, 19. (?) Died, Hoboken, April 20, 1864.

THOMAS EDDY, jun.

JOHN LE CONTE, Esq.,
> Age 33. Died November 21, 1860. See Botanical Gazette, VIII., 197.

PETER S. TOWNSHEND, M. D.,
> Columbia, 1812. Class of 1816, College of Physicians and Surgeons. Age, 22. Died, New York, March 26, 1849.

B. P. AYDELOTT, M. D.,
> Class of 1815, College of Physicians and Surgeons.

JACOB DYCKMAN, M. D.,
> Columbia, 1810. Class of 1813, College of Physicians and Surgeons. Died, at Kingsbridge, December 5, 1822.

JAMES CLEMENTS, Veterinary Surgeon.

SAMUEL B. CORNING.

WILLIAM S. IRVING.

HUGH MAXWELL, Esq.,
> Attorney and Counsellor, 61 Nassau street.

JAMES PIERCE,
> Shipmaster, 42 Water street.

WILLIAM H. CLARK.

BENJAMIN U. COLES,
> Flour Merchant, 1 South street.

Original Members

SAMUEL AKERLY, M. D.,
 Columbia, 1804. Brother-in-law of Samuel L. Mitchill.

JAMES SMITH, Esq.

WILLIAM CUMBERLAND,
 Carver and Gilder, 111 William street.

STEPHEN B. LEMOINE, Esq.,
 Attorney, 27 Wall street.

JOHN W. WYMAN, Esq.,
 Attorney, 2 Park Place.

DR. J. M. S. M'KNIGHT,
 5 Dey street.

The name of James S. Watkins should, it would seem, have been included here. Perhaps he was prevented by his sickness from signing the Constitution. He was a graduate of Columbia, 1815; a member of the Class of 1817, College of Physicians and Surgeons. Died, New York, June 6, 1817. Aged 20.

Corresponding Members.

BENJAMIN R. GREENLAND, M. D., S. Carolina,
 Class of 1817, College of Physicians and Surgeons.

M. D. L. F. ERVING, S. Carolina.

LEWIS C. BECK, Schenectady (N. York).

CHARLES C. TOWNSEND, S. Carolina.

J. ROANE, M. D., Tennessee,
 Class of 1817, College of Physicians and Surgeons.

B. R. OWEN, Tennessee,
 Probably a mistake for R. B. Owen, Class of 1818, College of Physicians and Surgeons.

CORNELIUS P. HEERMANS, M. D.,
 Class of 1817, College of Physicians and Surgeons.

HENRY S. DODGE, Esq.

C. S. RAFINESQUE.
>Born in Europe, 1784. Died, Philadelphia, 1842.

THEOD. R. BECK, M. D., Albany (N. York),
>First Graduate of College of Physicians and Surgeons, Class 1811. Age, 26. Died, Albany, November 19, 1855.

THOMAS HARRIS, M. D., Philadelphia.
HENRY MARSHALL, M.D., Delaware Cy. (N.York).
CAPT. —— DOUGLASS, West Point.
WILLIAM A. FANNING.
DAVID P. ADAMS, Esq.

Honorary Members.

GENERAL JOSEPH G. SWIFT.
WILLIAM J. MACNEVIN, M. D., New York.
SIR CHARLES HAMILTON SMITH, Antwerp.
ZACCHEUS COLLINS, Philadelphia.
BRACEY CLARK, Veterinary Surgeon, London.
REV. HENRY STEINHAUER, Bethlehem (Penn.).
BENJAMIN HOMANS, Esq., Washington City.
PROFESSOR EBELING, of Hamburg.
REV. MR. FREEHAUF, Nazareth (Penn.).
PROFESSOR SOMME, Antwerp.
H. CASSTROM, Esq., Stockholm.
HOFFMAN BANG, Esq., Odense (Denmark).
REV. E. NOTT, Pres. Union College, Schenectady.
STEPHEN ELLIOT, Esq., Charleston, S.C.

This first printed list of members is found among the bound papers of the Society. It contains all the

Original Members

names, either as Resident or Corresponding Members, which are comprised in the minutes of February 24th, excepting that of Lewis C. Townsend, and it contains several names which are not mentioned in the records. It should, however, be regarded as the most authoritative list.

Of the thirty-one Resident Members, at least twelve were connected with the College of Physicians and Surgeons, six being graduates, four being students, and two of them belonging to the faculty. Or, if we include Watkins, the proportion would be thirteen out of thirty-two. However, the fact that the Lyceum originated in the above named institution is better shown by a study of the names signed to the Constitution at the meeting of organization. There were twenty names affixed, judging by the minutes, and of these, thirteen were related to the College. At the time of the printing of the list of members, several of these had become Corresponding Members.

Another matter of interest is the ages of the members. Most of them were quite young men, some being under twenty years. Of those connected with the College (the ages of the other members are not known), the President was the only elderly man, he being fifty-three. The activity and enthusiasm of the young society may be explained by the youth of its members, and by the inspiring personal influence of Dr. Mitchill.

SECTION III.

Places of Meeting, and the Lyceum Building.

THE Society had its birth, as regards both the men and the place, in the College of Physicians and Surgeons, in Barclay street, near Broadway. With one exception all the meetings until April were held there. The exception is notable, as it was the meeting of organization, the first *Annual Meeting*. This was held in "Harmony Hall," February 24, 1817. (See page 5.)

"Harmony Hall" was "a public house," a two-story wood building on the southeast corner of Duane and William streets. It was a political headquarters and was used as a transient meeting-place for various organizations. At a later date it was rebuilt and named "The Shakespeare," and the site is now occupied by the Newsboys' Lodging House.

As soon as the new Society was fairly organized and known, it was offered quarters free of rent in the "New York Institution." (See page 12.) The first meeting there was held April 21, 1817, and the Society there abode until September, 1831.

The "New York Institution" was one of the landmarks of old New York. It was erected in 1795 for

COLLEGE OF PHYSICIANS AND SURGEONS
BARCLAY STREET

an almshouse, and occupied the site of the present City Court House, north side of City Hall Park, facing Chambers street. It was used as a home for the poor until 1816, and was ever after more commonly known as the "Old Almshouse." In 1816 the Common Council generously gave the use of the building to various societies, free of rent, for ten years.* Among the societies, besides the Lyceum, were the Historical Society, the Literary and Philosophical Society, and the Academy of Fine Arts.

The west end of the building was occupied by Scudder's "American Museum." In rooms adjoining those of the Lyceum Dr. John Griscom gave chemical and philosophical lectures.

The building was of brick, three stories high, with a basement, and with no claim to beauty. It was destroyed by fire many years later.

The LXVIII. canto of Halleck's poem "Fanny," written in 1821, refers to the building and its occupants:

> "And, therefore, I am silent. It remains
>   To bless the hour the Corporation took it
> Into their heads to give the rich in brains
>   The worn-out mansion of the poor in pocket,
> Once "the old almshouse," now a school of wisdom
> Sacred to Scudder's shells and Dr. Griscom."

In 1826 the Lyceum came out victorious from a contest with Dr. Griscom over rooms. The latter had occupied two rooms for lecture purposes for ten years. As the lease was expiring he neglected to apply to the Common Council for a renewal, although notified by

---
* See Pictures of New York and Strangers' Guide, N. Y., 1828.

the officers of the Lyceum that they wished to obtain the rooms, which adjoined those of the Lyceum and would consequently be very advantageous to the Society for museum purposes. At the proper time the Lyceum applied for and obtained a lease of Dr. Griscom's rooms, and asked him for the keys which, after conferences, he positively refused. The Curators then took forcible possession. Dr. Griscom appealed to the Common Council, and the Committee of Arts and Sciences of the Council gave a hearing to both parties. Dr. Griscom admitted that he had given only four lectures in the rooms during the last year, and that he had what he called an "evanescent intimation" that the Lyceum desired the rooms. But he had more apparatus there than he could dispose of, and he had thought the Corporation would not disturb him. The Committee made a somewhat sarcastic and minute report in favor of the Lyceum, which report, signed by Henry Arcularius and John Lozier, is copied into the minutes of the Lyceum.

After this the Society occupied at least four rooms. The Collections were displayed and on public exhibition.

The meetings of the Lyceum were held throughout the year. The summer vacation is a later invention, dating from 1844. The attendance at the meetings during all those years was very small, generally less than twelve. At this time the active men were Delafield, De Kay, Barnes, Graves, Torrey, Van Rensselaer, Cooper, J. A. Smith, Cozzens, Gale, Dana, Hoyt and Mitchill.

On April 27, 1829, the President read a summons

from the Corporation to vacate the rooms by August 1st. A movement was then inaugurated to raise money for a building.*

At the meeting of August 3, 1829, President Delafield announced that, in compliance with a resolution of the Common Council, he " had delivered the keys to the Mayor of the city, who had returned them, with the understanding that they were to be re-delivered to him when called for by the Corporation." The President and the Mayor immediately afterward made a written agreement to that effect, and the Society was permitted to use the rooms for more than a year thereafter. During this time propositions relating to a home for the Society were considered from several quarters, and different plans discussed. July 12, 1830, a resolution was adopted accepting a proposition from the University to the effect that, when the University should erect its new building, the Lyceum could have rooms free, on condition that the University should have free use of the Library and Collections. But the University had not found a location, and the Lyceum had need immediately of new quarters. November 1, 1830, another report was read from a Committee on Rooms, and a Memorial to the Corporation and the Public was printed, asking for the use of the " Rotunda," or other place, and the continued assistance of the public authorities. At the same meeting the President was authorized to ask the " Literary and Philosophical Society " for the temporary use of their rooms for the meeting of the Lyceum and the Library.

---

* The points bearing upon the " Broadway Building " and real estate will be found under that head, page 35.

On November 8th the subject of rooms was again considered, and the adjournment was to the rooms of the "Literary and Philosophical Society."

At the next meeting, November 15th, there was read some correspondence between the Lyceum and a Committee of the Council of the University, and the Rev. Dr. Mathews was present to speak for the University. The University authorities were desirous of a permanent connection with the Lyceum; and Dr. Mathews stated that while the University was waiting for its proposed new building, they would provide temporary quarters for the Lyceum at the expense of the University.

November 29, 1830, the Curators reported that the Committee on Public Offices of the Corporation had appropriated certain rooms, previously held by the "Savings Bank," for the temporary deposit of the collections. It was also reported that the Library was removed to the rooms of the Literary and Philosophical Society. During February and March, 1831, some of the collections, the "wet preparations," were deposited with Mr. Cozzens.

Upon April 25, 1831, Mr. Cozzens reported a written agreement with the Trustees of the "Dispensary" for rooms in their building at the corner of White and Centre streets, and the Curators were authorized to remove to that place the Cabinets and Library. May 2, 1831, a committee was appointed to prepare the rooms at the Dispensary; May 9th, Mr. Cozzens reported the removal of boxes, furniture, etc., and on August 1st he reported the rooms at the Dispensary in order. August 29th, business relating to the re-

NEW YORK INSTITUTION
The "Old Almshouse"
WESTERN END, FACING BROADWAY

moval to White street was transacted, and September 4, 1831, the minutes are dated at White street.

Among the old papers of the Academy there exists what seems to be the original lease spoken of by Mr. Cozzens. It is an old style form, signed by W. W. Fox and M. Field, Committee, stating that they had the "twenty-third day of March, 1831, let and rented unto the New York Lyceum of Natural History, the upper or third story of our building at the corner of White and Centre streets * * * * * for the term of one year and one month, to commence the first day of April, at the yearly rent of one hundred and fifty dollars, payable quarterly."

The rooms in the New York Dispensary were taken under the agreement with the University. A bill of rent was ordered, September 4th, to be sent to the University for payment. October 10th, the President said the University Trustees were to pay the rent; and a resolution was passed that official notice should be sent to the Trustees of the University that the Lyceum had taken rooms in the Dispensary, and an invitation extended to them to visit the new rooms; also a notice that the Lyceum would take quarters in the University building when it was ready.

November 26, 1832, a committee made a long and minute report "on the prospects of the Lyceum." The view taken was rather despondent. The uncertainty concerning a location, and dependent circumstances, was regarded as being an injury to the Society. It appears from this report that the rent was paid by the University, and that the Society was anticipating the time when it should have permanent rooms with that institution. A committee was appointed, pursuant to the recommendation of this report, to obtain information concerning the cost of ground and a building.

November 19, 1832, there was mention of a request by the New York College of Pharmacy for some sort of union in a building project. This plan was not seriously considered.

Another long report on ways and means was presented by a committee December 3d. From this report we learn that the paying membership for several years had been from forty to fifty.

December 24, 1832, a committee to confer with the Chancellor of the University reported that the University had a strong desire to continue the connection with the Lyceum, but that the Society should feel at liberty to do as it deemed best for its own interests. A committee was then appointed to purchase a lot, and another committee of six to solicit aid. James E. De Kay was apparently the most active spirit.

May 20, 1833, a committee was appointed with full power to procure the building of the "Female High School" for the Lyceum. At a later date a movement was made to reach the shareholders of that institution in behalf of the Lyceum; but upon October 7th the President said that he was informed that the building was promised to the "Mechanics' Institute."

There was also a suggestion or request received May 20th, from the President of Columbia College, that the Lyceum unite with the "Library and Athenæum" in erecting a building upon the college grounds. This proposition was not accepted. The society seems to have determined that it was possible for them to have a building entirely their own; and we cannot doubt that such was the wiser course.

The meetings were still nominally held all summer. But in 1834 a quorum was lacking from August 4th to September 15th, and during every summer thereafter many meetings were left without a quorum.

The Lyceum Building—Real Estate.

A REPORT of Committee was read and adopted April 27, 1829, which recommended the securing of a building-fund by subscriptions to building-stock, the shares to be $100 each, and the Lyceum to take fifteen shares. On May 11th a form of subscription paper was adopted. By this plan, which was finally successful, each share of $100 carried with it certain privileges, essentially equivalent to those of membership, save the right of voting. (See page 37.) The movement was not very active or effective, apparently, as the next important mention of the matter in the minutes is not until November, 1830. At the meeting of November 15, 1830, the matter of appointing a committee to purchase a lot was debated, and motion was lost by a vote of six to nine.

The next reference to building is on November 26, 1832, when a long report "on the prospects of the Lyceum" was read (see page 33), and a committee was appointed to determine the cost of lots and make other related inquiries.

December 24, 1832, a committee was appointed to

purchase a lot; and on February 18, 1833, this committee was authorized to buy a lot in Grand street; and the Treasurer was authorized to sell the stock held by the Lyceum and invest the proceeds in real estate.

Upon February 25, 1833, Dr. Van Rensselaer reported the purchase of a lot in Grand street for $5,000; and March 11th he reported the payment of $1,000 upon the lot.

A committee was appointed at this meeting, March 11th, to consider the subject of erecting a building upon the Grand street lot. Their report was presented March 25th, saying that the erection of a building was deemed expedient, as soon as funds could be procured, but that in the meantime the property should be rented.

December 22, 1834, the Treasurer was authorized to purchase ground on Broadway, between Houston and Prince streets; but December 29th he reported that the purchase was not made.

January 11, 1835, a committee was appointed to make inquiries concerning price, etc., of lots between Spring and Prince streets on Broadway.

January 19th the Treasurer reported the full payment of the mortgage on the Grand street lot; and the Committee appointed the week before reported the lots in question worth from $20,000 to $22,000. At the next meeting, January 26, 1835, a committee was appointed to purchase these lots.

At the meeting of February 2, 1835, Dr. John C. Jay, of the Purchasing Committee, reported the purchase, at auction, of one lot, 25x100 feet, for $11,000. This was the west side of Broadway, the third lot

NEW YORK DISPENSARY

WHITE AND CENTRE STREETS

south of Prince street. The Committee had also bought, at private sale, the lot adjoining southward, it being the same size, for the same price. The terms were ten per cent. on day of sale, thirty per cent. before the 15th inst., and the rest on mortgage at six per cent. The Committee recommended the sale of the Grand street lot, and the borrowing of money to pay in full for the two lots. These resolutions were adopted ; also a resolution to publish a pamphlet relating to subscriptions.

February 16, 1835, Dr. Jay reported an offer of a loan of $25,000—$15,000 upon the ground and $10,000 upon a building, to be worth ——, as soon as roofed. The Committee was authorized to accept the offer, and to fill the blank with $17,000, or $15,000 if possible.

The pamphlet ordered printed February 2d was now displayed. This has twenty-four pages. The first six pages are " REMARKS EXPLANATORY OF THE OBJECTS OF THE LYCEUM OF NATURAL HISTORY." Then follows the matter for which more particularly the pamphlet was published :

" TERMS OF SUBSCRIPTION TO THE STOCK OF THE LYCEUM OF NATURAL HISTORY IN THE CITY OF NEW YORK.

" *First.*—The stock to be divided into shares of one hundred dollars each.

" *Second.*—A stockholder to be entitled, for himself and family, to free admission to the Museum of the Society, and to such public lectures as may be delivered in its behalf, and to which the members of the Lyceum have a right to attend ; and also to have the privilege of introducing strangers to the Museum and Lectures, in accordance with the regulations.

" *Third.*—A stockholder to be entitled to the use of the books of the Library of the Lyceum.

"*Fourth.*—A member becoming a stockholder, to be exempted from the initiation fees, and to the annual payments due subsequent to the date of his subscription.

"*Fifth.*—The shares, with their privileges, may be transferred or bequeathed.

"*Sixth.*—The sum of five thousand dollars, exclusive of the Society's subscription, to be subscribed before the stockholders are liable for their shares."

The Lyceum is down for twenty-five shares. Then follow the names of eighty-nine persons who took one share each.

The Charter, Constitution and By-Laws make up the rest of the pamphlet.

At the meeting of February 16, 1835, a committee was empowered to procure plans and estimates for a building.

March 2, 1835, Dr. Jay reported full payment upon one lot from the subscriptions, and $1,100 paid on the other lot, with $900 due the Committee. And on date March 9, 1835, Dr. Jay reported the perfecting of the loan of $15,000, and the lots paid for.

The number of subscribers to the building fund, as reported by Dr. Jay on April 13th, was one hundred and twenty-eight. Two others were reported July 13th. The names of these subscribers are included in our later catalogue publications.

The "Building Committee," appointed May 4, consisted of Delafield, Jay, Cooper, H. W. Field and A. R. Thompson. Throughout the whole course of the enterprise Dr. John C. Jay was the leading spirit. May 11th he reported the excavation for the building as begun; July 11th a first payment of $1,000 was reported.

February 22, 1836, Dr. Jay made a report on the

"Building Fund." The receipts from all sources, including loan of $25,000, were $39,813. The expenditures were $37,774, which left a balance on hand of $2,038.

The Society met for the first time in its new building May 9, 1836. There were eighteen members present, an unusually large attendance.

*" This edifice would at the present day be considered a very contracted space for the library and collections of a Natural History Society. Nevertheless for that period it was in advance of any similar building in the land, far larger and more commodious than that occupied by its older sister society in Philadelphia. On each side of a spacious entrance hall were stores intended for rental. At the end of the hall was a lecture room of moderate size, with seats rising from the central platform. The front portion of the second and third stories was devoted to the Museum, which room was about 50 feet by 70, lofty and surrounded by a gallery. In the rear of the second story was a spacious and comfortable room for the library and for the ordinary meetings of the Society. Above these were the rooms for the Superintendent or Librarian and for the Janitor."

The Lyceum building was Nos. 561, 563, 565 Broadway. It had a frontage of 50 feet and a depth of nearly 100 feet. The cut of the building, which was used upon announcements and publications, fairly represents the front, which was of a light gray color, and the pilasters, at least, were of granite.

---

* This and other quotations marked (R) are from reminiscences kindly furnished the author by Mr. J. H. Redfield.

The elder Silliman was invited to dedicate the new building by a course of lectures on Geology, which were delivered upon evenings between January 5th and 17th, 1837. He was assisted in the preparation by Mr. Charles E. West, then a private pupil of the lecturer and afterwards an active member of the Lyceum. The controversy over the Mosaic cosmogony was beginning at this time, and the lectures produced great interest. For the course of seven lectures Silliman was paid $900.*

The first anniversary occasion (annual meeting) in the new building, February, 1837, was celebrated by an address from Dr. John W. Francis.

Upon July 4, 1837, Dr. Jay reported the borrowing of $5,000 on mortgage, which the meeting the preceding week had authorized. August 21, 1837, the Treasurer was authorized to borrow $2,200. These loans were probably from Dr. Jay himself, for from the minutes of September 3, 1838, it appears that Dr. Jay, the Treasurer, had himself loaned the Society $10,000, and he was then authorized to borrow to cancel his debt. The total debt was now $35,000.

Many items are found in the minutes relating to the renting of the stores and upper rooms. The stores were rented, some of the time, for $750 each yearly. Some rooms above were rented for $350 per year. The lecture room and the museum room were also made to add to the income. The lecture room was leased for use upon the Sabbath as a place of worship for the New Jerusalem Church, at $350 per year. At one time the museum room was rented for six months,

---
* From a private letter by Dr. Charles E. West, of Brooklyn.

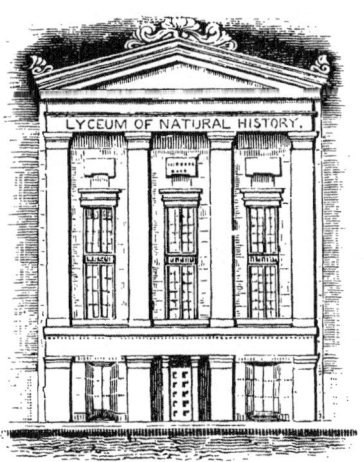

THE LYCEUM BUILDING

NO. 563 BROADWAY

for an exhibition of paintings, for $400. There were various offers, some of them accepted, to rent rooms temporarily or for periodical use.

The income seems, however, to have been insufficient. February 22, 1841, the Finance Committee was authorized to devise means of decreasing expenses and increasing the revenue.

February 7, 1842, it was resolved to reconstruct the lecture room so as to derive more money from it. February 6, 1843, an offer of $1,200 per year for the store and lecture room was accepted, as was also another of $550 per year for the museum room. The cases were moved into the gallery.

Early in 1843 it was apparent that financial trouble was impending. The ground had been purchased, and the building erected at great cost during a period of inflation and excitement. With the fall in values and the stagnation in business succeeding the speculative period, the Society was seriously embarrassed. Concerning this, Mr. J. H. Redfield writes:

" Next among the calamities was the financial disturbance which swept over the land after the inflation and speculative fever of 1836. The reaction from that inflation reached its height in 1839. In these days of plethora of capital, with money begging for four per cent. interest, we can hardly realize the severity of the monetary constriction of that period. All property seemed to have lost its value, and confidence was destroyed. I have already mentioned that the Lyceum's real estate was mortgaged for $35,000. The first effect of the stringency was to stop at once all subscriptions to the building fund. No more were to be found willing to invest $100, interest payable in lectures and library privileges. The stores, the rental of which was expected to pay the interest on the Society's debt, and to contribute to its reduction, remained unrented. It even became necessary to pledge the scientific collections of the Society for a further loan, which was, with difficulty, obtained from a friend of the institution." (See page 48.)

May 1, 1843, the Finance Committee reported the necessity of immediate action, and advised a meeting of the stockholders. Such a meeting was ordered May 22d. The only result seems to have been a resolve to appoint a subscription committee. The financial straitness of the time and the hopeless feeling of the members of the Society, are shown in the statement of the President, made July 3d, that he could not find men willing to serve upon such a committee.

The discouraged feeling prevented the meetings from having a quorum from August 14th to October 2d. Upon the latter date a letter was read from the solicitor of Wm. W. Pell, asking for $10,000, which was due September, 1842, and threatening foreclosure. The President then appointed a committee to solicit help. The committee reported no progress at the next meeting, October 9th. A letter from Dr. Jay was read, offering "to extend the time of his subscription if the Society would reduce the debt to $28,000." It was decided to advertise the building for sale, at a price not under $45,000. The building was so advertised between October 9th and 16th. November 6th the financial condition was such that there was trouble

The Lyceum Building 43

about some trifling bills. For four meetings, from December 11th, there was no quorum.

There was mention at the meeting of January 8, 1844, of an impending suit. January 15th, correspondence was read relating to postponement of sale of the building. A letter from Dr. Jay refused to consent to postponement of the sale, but offered to pay $500 to be released from his office of bondsman. He was liable for $35,000, and after February his liability would have been increased by interest, taxes, insurance, etc. Notice was given the tenants to remove their property.

February 19th the Lyceum was looking for rooms elsewhere, and Gibbs, Wheatley and Brevoort were appointed a committee to consider the future of the Society.

Special efforts were made to secure a large attendance at the meeting of February 26, 1844, with the result of the unusual number of twenty-one members present. This was due to the fact that three days previously the building had been sold at auction, and the Society was without a home. The bidding at the sale had been very sluggish, and as soon as the amount was sufficient to cover the mortgages with interest, the friends of the Society ceased bidding, and the property was sold for $37,000. " And the Lyceum found itself out of debt and out of a home, with a valuable library and large collections, and no place to put them."[R]

A portion of the Master's report is displayed in the minutes, which states that the building and lots were sold to Mr. Howland, under proceedings in favor of W. W. Pell, for $10,000, with interest at seven per cent. The first and second mortgages were for $15,000 and $10,000 in favor of P. Lorillard. These, with interest, amounted to $26,699.66. Mr. Pell's claim was not met by $1.18.

At this meeting, February 26, 1844, Professor Mason, of the University, also a member of the Lyceum, stated that the Society could have rooms on the north side of the University buildings, similar to those occupied by the Historical Society, but that the mortgage of $2,000 on the Library and Collections must first be removed. He promised to secure the funds and raise the mortgage if the Lyceum would appoint a committee. The meeting, by preamble and resolution, appointed a committee with power to raise the funds, arrange for apartments and remove the property.

March 4, 1844, Dr. Jay delivered into the hands of the new Treasurer, J. P. Giraud, the papers of his office and check for funds on hand of $443.66.

March 18th Professor Mason reported $440 subscribed. March 25th Mr. Cozzens reported some property and Mr. Cramer's boxes removed to the University. (See page 90.)

April 1, 1844, the Subscription Committee was authorized to remove the Library to the University. And with this meeting the Society took leave of the building, and a sad chapter in its history was closed.

In a few years all kinds of business grew brighter, and trade tended toward the upper part of Broadway. About 1867, the former property of the Lyceum was sold for $200,000. The forecast of Dr. Jay and those who planned the enterprise was fully justified. They

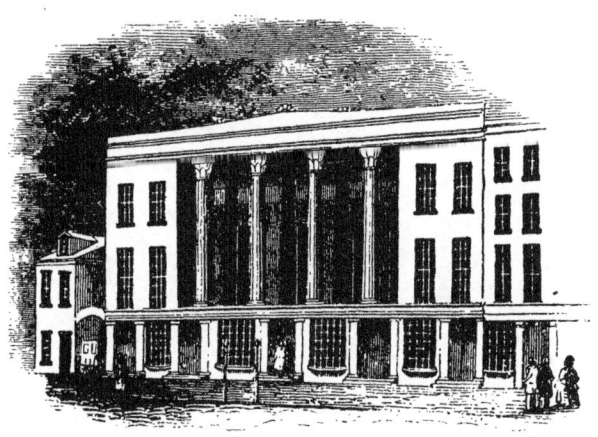

STUYVESANT INSTITUTE
UNIVERSITY MEDICAL COLLEGE

Places of Meeting 45

had "only made the common mistake of being a little ahead of time."[R]

In the crisis due to the loss of the building, the President, Major Joseph Delafield, then residing at No. 104 Franklin street, offered the Society the use of his library for the meetings. On Tuesday evening, April 9, 1844, the first meeting was held there, and for just one year the discouraged members there held their weekly talks. For the first time a summer vacation was formally voted, from July 9th to October.

October 17th the Committee reported the subscriptions as $1,100 to $1,200, and it was voted to ask payment when they amounted to $1,600.

During the winter the meetings sometimes failed of a quorum. January 30, 1845, Dr. Draper reported for Professor Mason that the subscriptions would reach $1,600 by the end of the week, and that the rooms at the University were vacant. Draper, Zabriskie and Redfield were made a committee to confer with the University officers.

At the meeting of February 6, 1845, the Rev. Professor Cyrus Mason said the building of the University Medical College on Broadway was under large liability to him, and he had the disposal of the entire front of the main story for ten years. He made the following offer to the Society:

"1. I will complete the subscription and pay off all the liabilities of the Lyceum.

"2. I will place the Lyceum in the three front rooms of the second story of the Stuyvesant Institute building, free of rent, for the term of ten years, and will provide fuel, light and servants' hire at my expense.

"3. To insure the fulfillment of the above arrangements, the

Lyceum to bind itself in the sum of $———— to remain the specified time."

This offer was provisionally accepted and a committee was appointed to take the necessary steps.

"The proposal was tempting and unexpected and to some members suspicious."(R) At the next meeting (February 13th) there was the remarkable attendance of twenty-four members. "Many of these were friends of the old College of Physicians and Surgeons. Dr. Torrey was among them. It soon appeared that old medical animosities were revived and that the Trojans of the 'Crosby Street School' feared the *Danaos et dona ferentes* of the newer establishment. No conceivable motive for such liberality could they see, unless to secure the prestige and reputation which might be derived from advertising the Lyceum of Natural History as part of their educational facilities; and fears were expressed that the professors of the new College would acquire the control and management of the Lyceum. The discussion was long and sharp—some things were said on both sides that would have been better unsaid—but finally a majority voted to accept the home that was offered them, whatever might be the risks."(R) A motion to reconsider the vote of acceptance of the preceding meeting was defeated by thirteen nays to eight ayes, and the favorable report of the Committee was referred back with instructions to include a clause by which either party could withdraw upon six months' notice.

At the next two meetings, with the large attendance of twenty-one at each, there was discussion over a form of contract. A disputed "6th section," retained at the first meeting, was, at the second meeting, replaced by another, in order to meet the views of the medical faculty. March 6th the agreement was approved and the officers directed to seal it, and the inevitable committee appointed to remove the property of the Lyceum from the University building to the Stuyvesant Institute.

The first meeting in the Stuyvesant Institute, 659 Broadway, opposite Bond street, was held Monday, April 7, 1845, with twelve present. The meeting had been advertised in the *Post* and the *Journal of Commerce*.

Of the new home Mr. Redfield writes: "Though the new quarters were contracted in comparison with those of the building we had lost, still the Library was well accommodated, and the best part of the Natural History Collections was displayed. The prestige which it was supposed would be given to the new college never amounted to anything, and any danger from the predominating influence of its professors was effectually prevented by a wrangle about the degree of publicity allowed to the sign-board of the Lyceum, in the course of which some of the over-zealous young members who leaned to the old college managed to so offend the professors of the new that the latter thenceforth took little or no part in the affairs of the Lyceum. All this was unfortunate. By accepting the lease we had disaffected one set of friends, and by the ungracious manner in which we treated our new hosts we had in a measure disaffected another set.

"Still, in spite of this untoward state of affairs, the Institution thrived. Its meetings were well attended and the scientific discussions were full of interest. Professors Loomis, Gale, and occasionally Draper and Hodge, Mr. Seely, Dr. Budd and others enlivened the meetings, and occasionally my father (W. C. Redfield) would give a talk upon meteorologic or geologic subjects."

During the summer of 1845, following the removal to the Stuyvesant Institute, the Society was still in trouble for want of money for current expenses. The mortgage upon the Library and Collections in favor of Dr. Jay was unpaid, and six months' interest due, and the claim was pressed. Professor Mason was called upon to redeem his promise. A subscription was started among the members to defray current expenses and to publish the Annals; Dr. Jay sent fifty dollars for each purpose. Finally, on October 13, 1845, it was announced that Professor Mason had paid the mortgage and that the Society was free from all encumbrance.

In 1850, in anticipation of the removal of the Medical College, another effort was made to secure $10,000, as the nucleus of a building-fund, eventually to reach $30,000. A little pamphlet then issued contains a circular letter, a plan of subscription, bearing date of February 22, 1850, and resolutions electing Hickson W. Field, J. Carson Brevoort and Robert L. Stuart, three trustees, to take charge of the funds; also a printed form for subscriptions. A few thousand dollars were subscribed, chiefly by Robert L. Stuart, Wm. C. Redfield and Major Delafield, not sufficient, however, to make the subscriptions binding.

The Society remained in the Stuyvesant Institute until March, 1851, when the Medical College sold the

UNIVERSITY MEDICAL COLLEGE
FOURTEENTH STREET

Places of Meeting

building and removed to their new edifice on Fourteenth street, upon the site of the present "Tammany Hall." The Lyceum was offered a meeting-room in the new college building, which was accepted. During the removal the Lyceum met at the house of Major Delafield, 104 Franklin street, from March 24th to June 30th. And after the summer vacation it met at W. C. Redfield's house, 338 Greenwich street, from September 8th to October 27th. The first meeting in the University Medical College building, in Fourteenth street, was November 3d. The requirements of the College left no room for the display of the Library and Collection of the Lyceum. The former was placed in the rooms of the Mercantile Library Association and most of the latter was packed in boxes and stored in the cellar of the College building.

In 1863 there was fruitless talk in regard to the erection of a building by Columbia College, upon its grounds, for the use of the Lyceum.

Another movement to secure a fund for the support of the Society was made in 1865. The circular letter explaining the plan has affixed to it the names of the active members of that time, which are these : William A. Haines, Robert L. Stuart, George N. Lawrence, J. Carson Brevoort, H. D. Van Nostrand, Charles A. Joy, Dr. John W. Greene, D. Jackson Steward, Charles M. Wheatley, Temple Prime, with Livingston Satterlee as chairman.

The effort was not successful, and subsequently several of the gentlemen above named threw their influence in favor of the projected American Museum of Natural History.

The loss of the Lyceum building in 1844 was a dispensation which might have taken all heart, and life even, from a society with any less steadfastness and resolution. However, the Collections and the Library were still intact, and the members were hoping for a time when they should have a home in which they could be permanently displayed.

But now there came another terrible calamity. On the night of May 21, 1866, the Medical College building, with all its valuable contents, was burned. The Collections of the Lyceum were not insured, and except the Library, the results of the enthusiasm, labor and sacrifices of half a century were gone. Well might the members have been entirely disheartened, even to the disbanding of the Society. But with characteristic persistence the organization and meetings continued. Through the courtesy of the Geographical Society, their rooms in Clinton Hall were used as a meeting place of the Lyceum for one year.

In 1867 the Society moved, with its Library, to the Mott Memorial Hall, No. 64 Madison avenue, where it continued until May 6, 1878.

Early in 1868 arrangements were made to take quarters in the Cooper Union building. Some delay occurred at the moment of removal, and, as a result, the plan was abandoned.

In 1876 the Lyceum changed its name to the NEW YORK ACADEMY OF SCIENCES, as is described in Section X. Upon the removal from Mott Memorial Hall the library was given a room in the American Museum of Natural History, where it remained until 1886. (See Section VII.)

HAMILTON HALL, COLUMBIA COLLEGE
BY PERMISSION OF D. APPLETON & CO.

From May 6, 1878, to October 1, 1883, the Society held its weekly meetings in the building of the New York Academy of Medicine, No. 12 West Thirty-first street.

Since October, 1883, the Society has been a recipient of the generosity of the Trustees of Columbia College, and has held its regular meetings in the Greek Lecture Room, in Hamilton Hall, and the lectures of the "Popular Lecture Course" in one of the large lecture rooms of the Library Building.

Dates of Removals.

1817, Organized in College of Physicians and Surgeons, Barclay Street, 2 mos.
1817, April 21, to 1831, Sept. 4, in New York Institution, - - 14 years.
1831, Sept. 4, to 1836, May 9, in New York Dispensary, - - 5 "
1836, May 9, to 1844, April 9, in Lyceum Building, - - - 8 "
1844, April 9, to 1845, April 7, in President Delafield's Library, - 1 year.
1845, April 7, to 1851, March 17, in Stuyvesant Institute, - - 6 years.
1851, March 24, to June 30, in President Delafield's House, - - 3 mos.
1851, Sept. 8, to Oct. 27, in W. C. Redfield's House, - - - 2 "
1851, Nov. 3, to 1866, May, in University Medical College in 14th St., 15 years.
1866, May, to 1867, in room of Geographical Society, Clinton Hall, - 1 year.
1867 to 1878, May 6, in Mott Memorial Hall, - - - - - 11 years.
1878, May 6, to 1883, Oct. 1, in New York Academy of Medicine, - 5 "
1883, Oct. 1, to present time, in Hamilton Hall, Columbia College.

SECTION IV.

Officers of the Society, 1817 to 1887.

Presidents.

	DATES OF ELECTION.
SAMUEL LATHAM MITCHILL,	1817–1823.
JOHN TORREY,	1824–1826, 1838.
JOSEPH DELAFIELD,	1827–1837, 1839–1865.
CHARLES A. JOY,	1866–1867.
JOHN S. NEWBERRY,	1868 to date.

First Vice-Presidents.

CASPAR WISTAR EDDY,	1817–1818.
FREDERICK C. SCHAEFFER,	1819–1821.
GEORGE GIBBS,	1822.
JOHN TORREY,	1823, 1834–1837, 1839.
DANIEL H. BARNES,	1824.
ABRAHAM HALSEY,	1825–1833.
JAMES E. DE KAY,	1838.
JOHN AUGUSTINE SMITH,	1840–1846.
JOHN LE CONTE,	1847–1851.

Officers of the Society 53

DATES OF ELECTION.

WILLIAM C. REDFIELD,	- 1852–1853.
WILLIAM COOPER,	- 1854–1864.
JOHN S. NEWBERRY,	- 1867.
GEORGE N. LAWRENCE,	- 1868.
THOMAS EGLESTON,	- 1869–1881.
BENJAMIN N. MARTIN,	- 1882–1883.
DANIEL S. MARTIN,	- 1884.
OLIVER P. HUBBARD,	- 1885 to date.

Second Vice-Presidents.

FREDERICK C. SCHAEFFER,	- 1817–1818.
SAMUEL AKERLY,	- 1819.
JOHN TORREY,	- 1820–1822, 1833.
DANIEL H. BARNES,	- 1823.
JAMES E. DE KAY,	- 1824, 1827–1832.
JOSEPH DELAFIELD,	- 1825–1826.
WILLIAM COOPER,	- 1834–1837.
JOHN AUGUSTINE SMITH,	- 1838–1839.
ABRAHAM HALSEY,	- 1840–1846.
WILLIAM C. REDFIELD,	- 1847–1851.
BERN W. BUDD,	- 1852–1853.
J. CARSON BREVOORT,	- 1854–1864.
LIVINGSTON SATTERLEE,	- 1867.
THOMAS EGLESTON,	- 1868.
WILLIAM A. HAINES,	- 1869.
BENJAMIN N. MARTIN,	- 1870–1871, 1875–1881.
PAUL SCHWEITZER,	- 1872.

DATES OF ELECTION.

HENRY MORTON,	1873–1874.
ALEXIS A. JULIEN,	1882–1883.
ALFRED C. POST,	1884.
WILLIAM P. TROWBRIDGE,	1885 to date.

Corresponding Secretaries.

JOHN W. FRANCIS,	1817 (declined).
JOHN LE CONTE,	1817 (absent).
SAMUEL AKERLY,	1817.
NATHANIEL PAULDING,	1818–1819.
PETER S. TOWNSEND,	1820.
JAMES E. DE KAY,	1821–1823.
JEREMIAH VAN RENSSELAER,	1824–1836.
SAMUEL THOMAS CAREY,	1837–1838.
JOHN H. REDFIELD,	1839–1860.
ROBERT DINWIDDIE,	1861–1875.
H. CARRINGTON BOLTON,	1876.
ALBERT R. LEEDS,	1877 to date.

Recording Secretaries.

JOHN B. BECK,	1817.
WILLIAM COOPER,	1818–1820.
ABRAHAM HALSEY,	1821–1823.
FREDERICK G. KING,	1824.
DANIEL H. BARNES,	1825–1826.
JOHN J. GRAVES,	1827, 1829, 1831.
LEONARD D. GALE,	1828, 1832.
ALFRED WAGSTAFF,	1830.

Officers of the Society

DATES OF ELECTION.

JAMES E. DE KAY,	1833.
SAMUEL T. CAREY,	1834–1836.
JOHN H. REDFIELD,	1837–1838.
ROBERT H. BROWNNE,	1839–1875.
OLIVER P. HUBBARD,	1876–1884.
HERMAN LEROY FAIRCHILD,	1885 to date.

Treasurers.

BENJAMIN P. KISSAM,	1817–1821.
LUCIUS BULL,	1822–1823.
WILLIAM COOPER,	1824–1835.
JOHN C. JAY,	1836–1843.
JACOB P. GIRAUD, JR.,	1844–1846.
CHARLES M. WHEATLEY,	1847–1863.
TEMPLE PRIME,	1864–1871.
JOHN H. HINTON,	1872 to date.

Librarians.

FREDERICK S. COZZENS,	1824.
JAMES E. DE KAY,	1825, 1828–1832.
JOHN J. GRAVES,	1826–1827.
JOHN C. JAY,	1833.
GEORGE W. BOYD,	1834–1835.
ASA GRAY,	1836.
ROBERT H. BROWNNE,	1837–1838, 1845–1848.
ISSACHAR COZZENS,	1839–1844.
ORAN W. MORRIS,	1849–1851, 1854–1867.
ROBERT DINWIDDIE,	1852–1853.

	DATES OF ELECTION.
ARTHUR M. EDWARDS,	1868, 1870–1872.
FERDINAND F. MAYER,	1869.
BERNARD G. AMEND,	1873–1875.
LOUIS ELSBERG,	1876–1883.
ALEXIS A. JULIEN,	1884 to date.

Councillors (of the Academy).

(THE OFFICERS OF THE ACADEMY, EXCEPTING THE LIBRARIAN, ARE EX-OFFICIO MEMBERS OF THE COUNCIL. SEE SECTION XII.)

ROBERT H. BROWNNE,	1876–1878.
CHARLES A. JOY,	1876.
GEORGE N. LAWRENCE,	1876–1885.
ALBERT R. LEEDS,	1876–1877.
DANIEL S. MARTIN,	1876–1883, 1885–1886.
HENRY MORTON,	1876.
ALFRED C. POST,	1877–1883.
TEMPLE PRIME,	1877.
ALEXIS A. JULIEN,	1878–1881, 1885–1886.
WILLIAM P. TROWBRIDGE,	1878–1884.
LOUIS ELSBERG,	1879–1884.
THOMAS EGLESTON,	1882–1883.
EDWARD H. DAY,	1884.
HERMAN L. FAIRCHILD,	1884.
CORNELIUS VAN BRUNT,	1884–1886.
JOHN MCDONALD,	1885.
JOHN J. STEVENSON,	1885–1886.
JOHN A. ALLEN,	1886.
P. H. DUDLEY,	1886.

Engraved by Gimber & Dick by Permission of the N.Y. Lyceum from a Painting by H. Inman.

SAMUEL. L. MITCHILL. M.D. L.L.D.

SECTION V.

Biographical Sketches.

Samuel L. Mitchill.

DR. SAMUEL LATHAM MITCHILL was at the time of the organization of the Lyceum a leading citizen, well known through the whole country, and perhaps the most eminent man of science in America. He had been active in political life, having been Congressman and United States Senator from the State of New York, and had been identified with many enterprises. He was then fifty-three years of age, and in the height of his reputation. The history of his life has been written by his associate, Dr. John W. Francis, and memoirs and sketches of him are easy to find.

Dr. Mitchill was born in North Hempstead, Queens Co., Long Island, August 20, 1764. He was a third son, and his parents were of the Society of Friends. He died in New York, September 7, 1831, at the age of sixty-seven.

While a youth he studied medicine with his uncle, Dr. Samuel Latham, and later in New York City with

Dr. Samuel Bard. He then spent four years in the University of Edinburgh, from which he graduated with honor as a Doctor of Medicine, and returned to America in 1786. His residence abroad only intensified his love for the land of his birth, then just emerging from the war for independence. With a desire to fit himself for the duties of public life in a republic, he studied law with Robert Yates, Chief Justice of New York.

In 1788 Columbia College gave him the honorary degree of A. M. From 1792 to 1801 he was Professor of Natural History, Chemistry and Agriculture in Columbia, and was Professor of Botany 1793 to 1795. While in the chair of Chemistry he published in America the system of Lavoisier, and became involved in a controversy with Priestley, which was, however, conducted with courtesy and ended in personal friendship.

The Society for the Promotion of Agriculture, Manufactures and Useful Arts was originated by Dr. Mitchill. Under this society he began in 1796 the mineralogical survey of New York. In 1798 he assisted Fulton and Livingston in the development of steam navigation.

In 1799 he married the daughter of Samuel Akerly, a noted shipbuilder, who had amassed a large fortune. He left no children, but his name is preserved through his brother's family.

In 1790 Dr. Mitchill was elected to the Legislature of New York, as an Assemblyman, from the place of his nativity, Queens County; and in 1797 was returned to the Assembly from the City and County of New York.

Biographical Sketches 59

In 1800 he was elected a Representative in the 7th Congress of the United States, and was reëlected to the 8th and 9th Congresses. November, 1804, he was appointed United States Senator by the Legislature of New York for five years, in place of John Armstrong, who was sent as Minister to France. At the close of his term as U. S. Senator, 1809, he was again sent to the State Assembly, and in 1810 was elected to the 11th U. S. Congress.

He was President of the Medical Society of the County of New York in 1807; and the same year was made Professor of Chemistry in the new College of Physicians and Surgeons. The next year he was changed to the Chair of Natural History, which place he filled for twelve years. It was during this time that he originated the *Lyceum of Natural History in the City of New York*, and gave it the help of his example and inspiring influence, as President, for seven years.

Under a reorganization of the College of Physicians and Surgeons, in 1820, he became Professor of Materia Medica and Botany, which chair he held until 1826, when the whole faculty resigned in a body, and he was elected Vice-President of the new Rutgers Medical College, 1826-1830.

For twenty years he was a physician of the New York Hospital. He was one of the originators of the New York Medical Repository and was its chief editor for sixteen years.

Through travel and associations he was intimate with most of the prominent Americans of his time; and his conversation and lectures abounded in reminiscence. He was a man of great versatility, a charming companion and an accomplished man of the world. As a publicist and a devotee of science, he was unrivaled among the New York men of his day.

Of scientific papers he published many, upon a great variety of subjects, especially upon Ichthyology. His style of writing was somewhat florid, abounding in figures and imaginative passages. He was a good classical scholar, and classical allusions are frequent in his writing.

One of the best examples of his brilliant style is the oration which he delivered at the celebration of the completion of the Erie Canal in 1825. This is contained in the memoir, commemorating that event, by Hon. C. D. Colden. Other examples, particularly his poetry, are in Duyckinck's Cyclopedia of American Literature.

The Library of the Academy contains a pamphlet, published by Mitchill, with the title: "Some of the Memorable Events and Occurrences in the Life of Samuel L. Mitchill, of New York, from the year 1786 to 1828." Two hundred and three items, enumerated chronologically, tell the story of a remarkable life. Many of these items are quoted in Duyckinck's Cyclopedia of American Literature.

A man of such nature and prominence was a bright mark for the pen of satire. We, however, observe that it was not unkindly in its spirit. Drake's poem in the "Croakers," "To the Surgeon-General of the State of New York," written in 1820, was addressed to Dr. Mitchill, who then occupied that newly created office. The last of the three stanzas is as follows:

Biographical Sketches

> " It matters not how high or low it is,
>   Thou knowest each hill and vale of knowledge,
> Fellow of forty-nine societies
>   And lecturer in Hosack's College.
> And when thou diest, for life is brief,
>   Thy name in all its gathered glory
> Shall shine, immortal as the leaf,
>   In Delaplaine's Repository."

The first part of the last stanza of "The Great Moral Picture," a satire upon the City Council, by Halleck, pays this tribute to his fame:

> " Time was when Dr, Mitchill's word was law,
> When monkeys, monsters, whales and Esquimaux
> Asked but a letter from his ready hand,
> To be the theme and wonder of the land."

Halleck's poem, " Fanny," refers also to Dr. Mitchill and the Lyceum. Speaking of " Fanny's father," in stanza CXLV.:

> " He once made the Lyceum a choice present
>   Of muscle-shells picked up at Rockaway;
> And Mitchill gave a classical and pleasant
>   Discourse about them in the streets that day,
> Naming the shells—and hard to put in verse 't was—
> ' Testaceous coverings of bivalve molluscas.' "

The Magazine of American History for September, 1886, in an account of the New York Historical Society, contains the following appreciative sketch:

" Dr. Mitchill was one of the most versatile and remarkable of men. * * * * * His medical career and scientific labors, as well as his political services and contributions to literature, gave him wide fame; he became in course of years an active member of nearly all the learned societies of the world. He was a sort of human dictionary, whose opinion was sought by all originators and

inventors of every grade throughout his generation. * * * * *
He was a polished orator, a versifier and a poet, a man of infinite humor and excellent fancy. His eccentricities furnished material for the wits of the day to fashion many a joke at his expense, over which no one laughed more heartily than himself. He was equally at home in studying the geology of Niagara or the anatomy of an egg; in offering suggestions as to the angle of a windmill or the shape of a gridiron; in deciphering a Babylonian brick or investigating bivalves and discoursing on conchology; and in advising how to apply steam to navigation or in disputing about the Bible with his neighbor, the Jewish rabbi. He possessed a charm of manner and a magnetism of mind that was unusual; and he did much to advance the public and private interests of America, and elevate our scholastic reputation in foreign countries."

In the later years of his life Dr. Mitchill was not active in the Lyceum; but his interest, sympathy and counsel were always to be relied upon. A large part of his valuable cabinet of natural history he donated to the Lyceum in 1826 (see Section VI.); and his collection of minerals, valued at $10,000, was given to the society by his widow.

He passed away crowned with honor and with the affection of his contemporaries. The members of the Academy cherish his memory as being the founder of the Society and the Nestor of American science.

PORTRAITS OF MITCHILL.

At the end of the pamphlet of events in Dr. Mitchill's life, referred to on page 60, the following occurs:

"The principal portraits of him are the following: One by Dunlap, in London, when he was quite young; one by Ames, in Albany; one by Boyle, in Washington; one by James, for Quebec; one by Jarvis, for himself, and one by Williams, for Boston. Another, done by Jarvis, and presented by him to the Literary and Philosophical Society, is considered a very good piece. Since that time Mr. Rembrandt Peale has executed a likeness which the connoisseurs pronounce to be admirable. There is one still later by Trott.

"A long time ago Scoles executed a small engraving of him from a pencil miniature by Weaver; and a very fine one has since been engraved by Durand, from an original by Jarvis. There is also a Lithographic print from Trott's picture, done by Imbert.

"A portrait executed by Lampdin, of Pittsburgh, and another by Parker, of Augusta, have been carried, it is said, to London. That by Inman is spoken of as an admired piece of painting. And a full length likeness by Parisen is now perparing for the Academy.

"OF BUSTS.—The ingenious *Mrs. Platt* once took his likeness in wax. Afterwards Coffee moulded one in clay. Then Professor *B. Dewitt* caused one in gypsum to be prepared for the College of Physicians and Surgeons, and more recently Browere has formed one of plaster in a very fine style."

The steel engraving used in this work was prepared for Herring's National Portrait Gallery subsequent to the date of the above writing. The original, the portrait by Inman, who was a pupil of Jarvis, is still owned by the Society, and is at present deposited in the Columbia College Library.

The engraving by Durand, above referred to, was on copper, and accompanies Dr. Mitchill's oration in Colden's Memoir of the Canal celebration of 1825. The Jarvis portrait which Durand copied was the one in the possession of the Literary and Philosophical Society, and it now hangs in the Library of Columbia College by the side of the Inman picture. It represents Dr. Mitchill in the red cape of a Doctor of Laws of the University of Edinburgh. The Durand engraving makes the forehead somewhat too high and expansive, and the eyes slightly too large and open; but, like the painting, it shows a younger man and fuller face than the Inman portrait and its copy herein used.

The engraving by Scoles, above mentioned, is a small etching on copper, a profile within a medallion. It shows a round, full face with prominent aquiline nose. Beneath the medallion was afterward engraved a vignette, designed by Dr. Alexander Anderson, following a suggestion to him by Dr. Mitchill himself, representing Cupid wrestling with Pan. This plate was used to illustrate Lossing's Memorial of Dr. Anderson.

A copy or duplicate of the Jarvis portrait is in the possession of Dr. Mitchill's relatives in New York, who also have another portrait of unknown authorship.

The New York Hospital has a portrait by Jarvis, but with a plain coat instead of the cape; also a copy presented by Dr. Budd, of the Inman portrait.

The portrait by Peale is now in the Academy of Natural Sciences of Philadelphia.

Joseph Delafield.

MAJOR JOSEPH DELAFIELD was born in New York City, August 22, 1790. His early youth was passed in New York and at his father's country seat, "Sunswick," upon which the village of Ravenswood was afterwards built, and which is now included in the limits of Long Island City. He was graduated at Yale College in 1808, and the same year commenced the study of law in the office of Josiah Ogden Hoffman. He was admitted to practice October 29, 1811, and was at the same time taken into partnership by Mr. Hoffman. He was appointed Lieutenant of the Fifth New York State militia March 12, 1810, and Captain of drafted militia February 4, 1812. On December 29, 1812, he received his commission of Captain in the United States service and served with Hawkins' regiment. His commission as Major of the 46th Regiment, United States Infantry, is dated April 15, 1814, and was issued under the most flattering circumstances.

MAJOR JOSEPH DELAFIELD.

Born August 22, 1790. Died February 12, 1875.

At the close of the war he resigned from the army. His friends urged him to resume the practice of the law, in which already he had distinguished himself; but he wished to lead a more active life, and accepted the appointment of Agent, and later of Commissioner, of the United States under the Treaty of Ghent for settling the northern boundary of the United States. From 1817 to 1828 his summers were passed in command of the several expeditions on the boundary, extending from the State of New York to the Lake of the Woods. It was at this time that he commenced the formation of his afterwards famous collection of minerals. Truly has it been written that "the Science of Mineralogy, which he loved so well, owes a debt of gratitude to Major Delafield which ought never to be forgotten."

He was a member of the Lyceum of Natural History from 1823 until his death, in 1875, and was President from 1827 to 1866, with the exception of one year (1838); his term of service, thirty-eight years, in one office being unequaled in the history of the Society. During the year succeeding the loss of the building President Delafield, then living at 104 Franklin street, generously gave the Lyceum the use of his library-room as a meeting-place; and in every way he was loyal to the Society through all the troubles, which were not few, that befel it during his presidency.

As a presiding officer, Major Delafield was very popular and much admired, and was eminently in his place. Born for command and leadership, his military experience gave added grace to a naturally dignified and courtly bearing. To his power of controlling other wills was happily united an amiable and conciliatory disposition. "All who are familiar with the history of that period (the close of the war of 1812) know the intense bitterness and party feeling that prevailed. Major Delafield's rare qualities of temper, judgment and moderation then became conspicuous. His professional abilities were constantly employed in courts-martial, and his tact, conciliation, and impartial temper were invoked to adjust quarrels and avert duels. He carried that same pacific temper through life; it was a part of his nature and came easily. He was amiable from disposition as well as principle—the pacificator of his social circle. * * * * That delicate tact has healed many a feud and reconciled many estranged friends." *

Major Delafield's accomplishments were varied, and his scientific attainments considerable, although he published very little. His excellent mineralogical cabinet, the finest of its time in New York, was willed to the Lyceum whenever they could give it suitable accommodations. He was a member of many scientific societies, foreign and American; a founder and trustee of the Athenæum, afterwards united with the Society Library, of which he was a trustee for many years; a trustee of the College of Physicians and Surgeons, vestryman of Trinity Church, etc. During the latter part of his life Major Delafield interested himself in improving his country seat on the Hudson River, about a mile north of Spuyten Duyvel, and known as "Fieldston."

At the time of his death he was one of three surviv-

---
* Memorial Sermon by Rev. Dr. Sullivan H. Weston.

ing brothers out of an eminent and honored family of nine boys and four girls. He died in New York, February 12, 1875, in his eighty-fifth year, retaining all of his faculties and much of his bodily strength until the last. His brothers, Henry and Dr. Edward Delafield, died successively on the two following days, and February 16th the three brothers were together buried from Trinity Church. It was a spectacle "that for impressive solemnity was never before seen in our populous city; there were borne up the crowded aisles of that cathedral the remains of three brothers who had died within three days of each other. * * * * The deceased had passed the allotted period of three score years and ten, and came down to the grave like shocks of corn fully ripe unto the harvest."*

In memory of their late President, the Lyceum of Natural History, at the meeting held March 22d, 1875, expressed their appreciation of the loss which they had sustained by the following resolution :—

COPY OF RESOLUTIONS ADOPTED BY THE "LYCEUM OF NATURAL HISTORY IN THE CITY OF NEW YORK" AT A MEETING HELD ON MONDAY EVENING, 22D MARCH, 1875.

Whereas, Our Heavenly Father, in Whose hands are the destinies of all mankind, has taken to Himself Joseph Delafield, for fifty-two years a member of the "Lyceum of Natural History," and for nearly forty years its honored President; therefore

Resolved, That we tender to the family of the deceased our sincere sympathy in their sad bereavement; that we express to them the profound respect entertained by the Lyceum for the learning which our late brother brought to its deliberations, for the impartiality with which he presided at all meetings, for the courtesy which characterized his dealings with his associates, and for the

---

* Memorial Sermon by Rev. Dr. Sullivan H. Weston.

example he has left us of the manners of a refined Christian gentleman.

Resolved, That a copy of these resolutions be communicated to the family of our late associate and that they be entered upon the minutes.

(Signed)   ROB'T. DINWIDDIE,
Corresponding Secretary,
Lyceum of Natural History.

The engraving of Major Delafield is from an admirable portrait, by Huntington, in the possession of the family, who also possess a miniature by Rogers.

John Torrey.

DR. JOHN TORREY, the second President of the Lyceum, and the last one surviving of its Original Members, was only nineteen years old when the Society was founded, and did not take his degree from the College of Physicians and Surgeons until the next year. He was one of the young men to whom the Society owed its enthusiasm and activity.

Dr. Torrey was born in New York, August 15, 1796. Of his early years little is known. His disposition was so modest and unassuming that little could ever be learned from him about himself. But his leaning toward the study of nature was established early, and at the time of the founding of the Lyceum he was recognized as a rising naturalist. Within less than three months from the organization of the Lyceum young Torrey was made one of a committee of three to prepare a "Catalogue of plants growing spontaneously within thirty miles of the city of New

York." The Committee reported December 17, 1817. This report was doubtless based upon the observations and notes of former years. It was printed at Albany, in 1819, and has always been recognized as Torrey's work. Even to this day it is a model of its kind, and of value for reference.

The members of the Torrey Botanical Club celebrated the semi-centennial of the presentation of this list, in a dinner at the Astor House, December 20, 1867.

In 1823 Yale conferred upon him the honorary degree of A. M.; Williams College, in 1825, gave him the degree of LL.D., as did also Amherst in 1845.

While Dr. Torrey's fame rests chiefly upon his botanical work, this was not his only labor or even his profession. He early abandoned the practice of medicine, as unsuited to his taste, and devoted himself to scientific teaching and study; chemistry being nominally his branch. The following are the positions which he occupied:

Professor of Chemistry, Geology and Mineralogy in the U. S. Military Academy at West Point, 1824-1827.
Professor of Chemistry and Botany in the College of Physicians and Surgeons, 1827-1855.
Emeritus Professor of the same, 1855 until death.
Professor of Chemistry and Natural History in the College of New Jersey, 1830-1854.
Chief Assayer of the United States, 1853-1873.
Botanist of the Geological Survey of the State of New York from 1836.

Dr. Torrey was a voluminous writer and author. His great projected work on the Flora of the Northern and Middle States was abandoned, after the publication of the first volume in 1824, and a compendium in 1826, on account of the change from the Linnæan to the natural system of classification.

The Herbarium and botanical library, upon which Dr. Torrey had expended forty years of loving labor, he presented in 1860 to Columbia College, where they remain, a monument to his name and fame.

Dr. Torrey was a member of many societies; but the Lyceum of Natural History, which he helped to found, and of which he was President, 1824 to 1826, inclusive, and again in 1838, was the one with which he was closely identified.

He held office in the Lyceum as follows :

Curator, 1817 and later.
Second Vice-President, 1820–1822, 1833.
First Vice-President, 1823, 1834–1837, 1839.
President, 1824–1826, 1838.

The Botanical Club which perpetuates his name originated in a semi-social weekly gathering of congenial spirits at his house, which meetings were held several years before organization.

His fatal illness kept him from the meeting of the Club at which the charter was adopted. He died March 10, 1873, at the age of 77, with the admiration and affection of a large circle of devoted friends. He had been a member of the Lyceum for 60 years.

William Cooper.

THE honor of having the longest intimate relation with the Lyceum belongs to William Cooper. The history of his life is closely identified with the history of the Society. He was one of the Original Members, and his connection with the Society covers a period of forty-seven years. Of that honored company only Dr. Torrey survived him; but Dr. Torrey's active relation with the Lyceum ended in 1839.

Mr. Cooper's father was of an English family, and his mother was a Miss Graham, of Ulster County, N. Y. The exact date of his birth is unknown, but it was about 1798. At the time of the formation of the Lyceum he was, therefore, nineteen (?) years old—one of the youngest of that youthful company. Torrey was but little his senior, and the two were close companions in those days, and fast friends during life. He helped Torrey in the latter's botanical work, and in later years Torrey dedicated to Cooper his "Compendium of the Flora of the Northern and Middle States," "as a testimony of respect for his attainments as a naturalist, and as an expression of high esteem for his virtues."

Following the advice of Dr. Mitchill he went to Europe, in 1821, to study Zoölogy, and spent nearly three years in museums and lecture-rooms and in the company of European naturalists; and he was the first American to receive the honor of an election to the London Zoölogical Society.

Being financially comfortable, Mr. Cooper devoted his life to Natural History. The early volumes of the "Annals" contain some of the results of his labors. His first work was upon Vertebrate Palæontology, at that time a comparatively uncultivated branch. He discovered the extension into the United States of the post-tertiary mammalian fauna of South America.

He was not a voluminous writer. With exceeding modesty, and being, perhaps, over cautious in naming new species, he generously permitted others to use his material, and sometimes to gain the credit that might have been his own. The naming of "Cooper's Hawk" is an illustration. Cooper shot the original specimen in Hudson County, N. J., but with his usual caution left it for Bonaparte to name—*Falco Cooperi*. He was an intimate friend of Bonaparte and assisted him in the preparation of his works, editing for him the last two volumes. The results of Cooper's work in Ornithology are largely incorporated in these volumes of Bonaparte. He also assisted Audubon and Nuttall and gave De Kay the use of his material in preparing the Zoölogy of the New York State Reports.

His delicate health prevented Mr. Cooper from abundant work in the field. Among his excursions, in those days of slow travel, was one to the "Big-bone Lick" in Kentucky. The collections which he there made went to the Lyceum, with other material.

In 1838 he retired to a farm at Guttenberg, N. J., on the shore of the Hudson, becoming a Corresponding Member. He removed to Hoboken in 1853, and resumed his attendance and Resident Membership at the Lyceum. At this time he began the collection in Conchology which went eventually to the Chicago Academy of Sciences; in this pursuit he made numerous dredging excursions, as far north as Nova Scotia and south to the Bahama Islands. His last article was a preliminary report on the shells of the west coast of North America, in the Pacific R. R. Reports.

It will be seen from the following list of offices held

Very truly yours
Jno. Cooper

by Mr. Cooper in the Lyceum, that he was the first Recording Secretary of the *chartered* Society ; and, except during the short absence in Europe and the longer residence in New Jersey, he was continually in office until his death. And his membership was unbroken.

    Recording Secretary, - - - - 1818–1820.
    Treasurer, - - - - - - - 1824–1835.
    Second Vice-President, - - - 1834–1837.
    First Vice-President, - - - - 1854–1864.

Mr. Cooper died April 20, 1864, and there passed away a respected and beloved citizen, an honored devotee of science, a gentle, retiring, unambitious, unselfish and pure spirit.

Dr. James G. Cooper, of California, who has been a member of the society for thirty years, is a son of William Cooper. A memorial of his father has been published by Dr. Cooper and his sister, to which the author of this sketch is largely indebted.

Robert H. Brownne.

THE Society owes a debt of gratitude to Robert H. Brownne that no tribute of words can attempt to pay. For thirty-seven consecutive years he performed the exacting duties of Recording Secretary, a length of continuous service exceeding that of any other officer, and the office the most laborious and imperative in its duties. This period was from 1839 to 1876, covering the time of discouragement due to the loss of the Building, the burning of the Collections and the frequent removals. In his quiet, modest way he kept the machinery of the Society in motion, and probably to him belongs the greatest credit of preserving the Lyceum during those years of trial. With unwearied patience, labor and self-sacrifice he kept the Records with admirable care and nicety all those many years. The painstaking precision of his work shows the utmost conscientiousness, while the labor involved proves his unfaltering love for the Lyceum. The unselfishness of his work, in this unpaid office, under such discouraging circumstances and for so many years, is heroic. It is another bright example of devotion to science, without fame or expectation of reward.

Mr. Brownne was elected to the Lyceum in 1833, being then twenty-three years old. He served as Librarian two years previous to his election to the Secretaryship in 1839; so the total length of his unbroken service as an officer is thirty-nine years. Moreover, from 1845 to 1849 he was again Librarian.

The following sketch of his life is taken, by permission, from the Bulletin of the Torrey Botanical Club, Vol. VI., p. 291, contributed by Mr. Redfield:

"We have to mourn the loss of an ardent lover of botanical science in the death of Robert H. Brownne, which occurred February 15, 1879, by apoplexy. He was born in this city, August 3, 1810. His father was a prominent shipbuilder in the earlier part of the century, being the head of the firm of Brownne & Bell, who modeled and constructed for Robert Fulton the 'Clermont,' the first steamboat which navigated the Hudson River. Young Brownne had an ardent thirst for knowledge, and made good use of the advantages which he enjoyed at the New York High School, in which he was educated, and in which he for many years held a position as teacher. That institution was then under the charge of Dr. John Griscom and Rev. Daniel H. Barnes, both of them men of solid learning, 'apt to teach,' and well versed in physical and natural science, which, previous to this period, had been little taught in schools. Their enthusiasm in this direction, and their personal magnetism, gave most of their pupils a decided bent toward the study of Nature. In early life Mr. Brownne was threatened with pulmonary disease, for which his physician prescribed active exercise in the open country. With the predilection acquired at school, it is not strange that he should now be led to take up botanical study as an additional incentive to the regimen prescribed.

"In 1833 he was elected a member of the New York Lyceum of Natural History, and in 1837 he became its Recording Secretary, and continued to hold that office until a few years previous to his death. At the time of his entrance into the Society its leading botanical members were Dr. Torrey, John Carey, Samuel T. Carey and Abraham Halsey, to whom soon after was added Dr. Asa Gray, now so preëminent. Brought into constant association with such men, Mr. Brownne could not fail to profit by their fellowship, and he became thoroughly versed in the botany of the Northern and Middle States. But his attainments were not limited to that field. He acquired a good knowledge of geology, mineralogy and conchology. His reading became extensive, and his acquaintance with bibliography and numismatics was not often excelled.

"After the dissolution of the New York High School he was appointed Principal of the Parochial School of the Scotch Presbyterian Church, which position he held to the day of his death. His reputation as an expert in mineralogy, conchology, bibliography and numismatics gave him wide employment in the work of arranging and cataloguing collections and libraries. For the last twenty-five years he acted as librarian for Robert L. Stuart of this city. He was also Secretary of the North-western Dispensary. Modest and unassuming in manner, with every solid virtue and Christian grace, his memory is precious to those who knew him."

William C. Redfield.

"A LIFE passed in the ordinary walks of business or in the quiet of philosophic research affords little of that romantic incident which lends a charm to biography; still we think the life of Mr. Redfield affords an interesting and instructive theme for contemplation in a threefold point of view: as affording a marked example of the successful pursuit of knowledge under difficulties; as happily illustrating the union, in the same individual, of the man of science with the man of business; and as exhibiting a philosopher whose researches have extended the boundaries of knowledge and greatly augmented the sum of human happiness."

The quotation above is from a beautiful tribute to the memory of Mr. Redfield, presented by Professor Denison Olmstead before the American Association for the Advancement of Science, at the Montreal

Biographical Sketches 77

meeting in 1857, and from which the matter of this sketch is chiefly taken.

Mr. Redfield was born in Middletown, Conn., March 26, 1789, of English ancestry. At the age of thirteen his father died, and the next year he was apprenticed to a mechanic. His education as a boy was limited to the common schools, very rudimentary in those days, and slight opportunity for study was found during the exacting apprenticeship. "These brief opportunities, however, he most diligently spent in the acquisition of knowledge, eagerly devouring every scientific work within his reach."

Professor Olmstead describes vividly how young Redfield, at the close of his apprenticeship, made a foot journey of over seven hundred miles, largely through an untracked wilderness, to see his mother, then removed to Ohio, returning in the same manner by a more southern route the following year. His observations upon those journeys were so fully and accurately recorded that in later years they were useful to him in planning the "Great Western Railway." In this performance we see manifested some of the elements of the strong and lovely character which made his life so useful.

"Returning to his former home in 1811, Mr. Redfield commenced the regular business of life. No circumstances could seem more unpropitious to his eminence as a philosopher than those in which he was placed for nearly twenty years after his first settlement in business. A small mechanic in a country village, eking out a scanty income by uniting with the products of his trade the sale of a small assortment of merchandise, Mr. Redfield met with obstacles which, in ordinary minds, would have quenched the desire of intellectual progress. Yet every year added largely to his scientific acquisitions, and developed more fully his intellectual and moral energies."

" Before the scientific world Mr. Redfield has appeared so exclusively in the character of a philosopher, especially of a meteorologist, that they have been hardly aware of the important services he has rendered the public in the character of *naval engineer*, particularly in the department of steamboat navigation." He " was the first to devise and carry into execution the plan of a line of *safety barges* to ply on the Hudson between New York and Albany." In 1826 he established the "Steam Navigation Company," and "the fleets of barges and canal boats, sometimes numbering forty or fifty, which make so conspicuous a feature on the Hudson River, were thus set in movement by Mr. Redfield, and for thirty years the superintendence of the line first established constituted the appropriate business of our friend." Into the conduct of this work he carried the scientific spirit in a remarkable degree, as is attested by the many papers and letters which he published relating to engineering topics.

Mr. Redfield " was the first to place before the American people the plan of a system of railroads connecting the waters of the Hudson with those of the Mississippi. His pamphlet containing this project, issued in 1829, is a proud monument of his enlarged views, of his accurate knowledge of the topography of the vast country * * * and of his extraordinary forecast. * * * * * * The route proposed is substantially that of the New York and Erie Railroad, as far as this goes; but his views extended still further, and he marked out, with prophetic accuracy, the course of the railroads which would connect with the Atlantic States the then infant States of Michigan, Indiana and Illinois." "At the moment when the Erie Canal, having just been completed, was at the summit of its popularity, Mr. Redfield set forth in his pamphlet, under nineteen distinct heads, the great superiority of railroads to canals, advantages which, although then contemplated only in theory, have been fully established by subsequent experience."

Mr. Redfield is credited with great influence in originating the Harlem, the Hartford and New Haven, and the Hudson River Railroads.

"The attention of Mr. Redfield was first drawn to the subject of storms in the year 1821, by examining the position of trees prostrated by the great September gale of that year. "On tracing further the course and direction of prostrated objects, and comparing the times when the storm reached different places, the idea flashed upon him that the storm was a *progressive* whirlwind. A conviction thus forced upon his mind, after a full survey of the facts, was not likely to lose its grasp. Amid all his cares it clung to him, and was cherished with the enthusiasm usual to the student of Nature, who is conscious of having become the honored medium of a new revelation of her mysteries. Nothing, however, could have been further from his mind than the thought that the full development of that idea would one day place him among the distinguished philosophers of [his] time."

He was so engaged in engineering enterprises th[at] it was not until 1831 that, at the solicitation [of] Professor Olmstead, he published in the Americ[an] Journal of Science the first of a long series of essa[ys] upon rotary storms, which have chiefly given him [his] scientific fame.

Mr. Redfield joined the Lyceum in 1837, and co[n]tinued an interested and active member until [his] death, February 12, 1857, at the age of sixty-eig[ht]. His business cares kept him from occupying any offi[ce] which demanded time and labor, but he was Seco[nd] Vice-President from 1847 to 1852, and First Vi[ce] President from 1852 to 1854. Subsequent to t[he] publication of his theory of storms he became co[n]nected with many home and foreign scientific societi[es]. He was the first President of the American Associati[on] for the Advancement of Science, the meeting bei[ng] held in Philadelphia in 1848; and the present bro[ad] plan of the Association was first proposed by hi[m]. Yale College conferred on him in 1839 the honora[ry] degree of Master of Arts.

"Three distinguishing marks of the true philosoph[er] met in William C. Redfield—originality to devise n[ew] things; patience to investigate; and logical powers [to] draw the proper conclusions. * * * * Few m[en] have given more signal proofs of an original, inhere[nt] love of knowledge. Whether we contemplate t[he] apprentice boy after the toils of the day, seeking [for] knowledge by the dim light of an open fire; or t[he] father of a young family, through dark scenes

yours truly
Wm C. Redfield

domestic affliction and mournful bereavements, still adding largely year by year to his intellectual stores; or the man of business in the whir of the great metropolis, loaded with onerous and responsible cares, giving every interval of leisure and the seasons chiefly employed in pleasure or repose to the study of the laws of Nature, * * * * we observe in all a mind in love with truth, ever searching and ever expanding. In society he was courteous, sincere, upright and benevolent; in his family tender, affectionate, wise in counsel and pure in example; in all his walk and conversation, and especially in the church of God, a devout and humble Christian."

Benjamin N. Martin.

BENJAMIN NICHOLAS MARTIN was born at Mount Holly, N. J., October 20, 1816, and died at his home in New York City, December 26, 1883. His father, John Peter Martin, originally of South Carolina, had served honorably and actively in the patriot army throughout the Revolutionary War. The subject of this sketch was his youngest son, who, after fitting for college at the old Trenton Academy, went to Yale, and entered the distinguished class of 1837, which has given to the country so many eminent names.

Professor Martin always felt, and with justice, that he had been led by more than human wisdom in his determination to study at New Haven rather than at Princeton. The choice directed his whole career.

Here began his life-long interest in scientific pursuits, under the lectures of Silliman, Olmsted and Shepard. Here he became spiritually impressed, and devoted his life to the service of the Gospel. Here he gained the strong, philosophical training, under the eminent Dr. Taylor, that made him so clear and so broad and so logical in his varied range of subsequent studies.

After some ten years of life as a preacher and pastor in Massachusetts and New York, Dr. Martin found himself without a charge, in Albany, N. Y. Here he spent the middle years of the century, studying, writing and preaching. Always fond of science, yet his chosen field had heretofore been metaphysics and theology, in which departments he had prepared many able articles and reviews. Here, however, the association with scientific friends at the State capital aroused anew his tastes in that direction, and he began actively writing and studying in natural history, geology and ethnology.

In 1852 he was invited to the chair of Philosophy and Literature in the University of this city, and at once entered on the position which he filled with so much happiness, success and honor during the thirty-one years of his after life. His great power lay in two things—his uncommon breadth of scholarship and his clearness and grasp of thought. These, joined with great freedom and cordiality of intercourse, and a lofty purpose of Christian usefulness, made him among all his students a master, a father and a guide.

Such a man naturally felt interest in the work of the Lyceum. He joined it in 1868, and was ever afterward a constant attendant at its meetings. He soon became active in the Society; and his marked personality impressed itself strongly on the membership. After the reorganization, in 1876, he was at once chosen to the Council, of which he was a highly valued member as long as he lived. In 1870 he was chosen Second Vice-President, and in 1882 First Vice-President, until the time of his death.

As a debater, or a presiding officer, Dr. Martin made a strong impression. His wide range of studies, his penetrating insight into principles, his ready sympathy and his union of gentleness with power could not but reveal him as a remarkable man. Whenever he rose to address the Society he was listened to with marked attention and respect. None who saw and heard him can ever forget that presence. The small, erect figure; the noble, scholarly head; the brilliant eyes; the flowing, silvery hair—at once attracted notice; while many persons have spoken with especial admiration of his singularly perfect and elegant English and his easy grace of manner and carriage.

Dr. Martin loved science in all its branches; but his deepest interest in it arose from its relations with moral and spiritual truth. He was a living and powerful witness to the "harmony of scientific and religious thought." All his latest and ripest work lay in that direction, and it was marked by great originality and force. Repeatedly, in the public lecture courses of the Academy, has he presented subjects of this kind, and always with eminent ability. "The Natural Theology of the Doctrine of the Forces," "The Moral Bearing of Recent Physical Theories," "Evidences of Design in the Original Structure of the Universe," and the like, were among these discussions; and in his last illness it is a striking fact that a mingled current of scientific and spiritual thought flowed through his brain and expressed itself in broken and wandering utterances. He died, as he had lived, a clear-sighted and joyous soul, strong in the faith of the Gospel, rich in the acquirements of knowledge, happy in the consciousness of work well done, and blessed in the vision of eternal life and ever-widening faculties in the service and kingdom of God.*

Personal Reminiscences, by J. H. Redfield.

"I WELL remember that when I first entered the Society (1836) I was rather oppressed with a sense of the profound learning of the circle to which I had been admitted, and felt that as a mere tyro I had made a mistake in intruding myself into so erudite a body of savants. But as I gradually became acquainted with the individual members and found them all, even those who were most learned, so genial, affable and unassuming, so ready to impart knowledge and to enlighten the ignorance of the novice, those feelings of diffidence soon wore off.

And here I am tempted to record my impressions and recollections of the leading members at this period. The President was Major Joseph Delafield, the First Vice-President was Dr. John Torrey, the Second Vice-President was William Cooper, the Corresponding Secretary was Jeremiah Van Rensselaer,

---

*A memorial notice of Prof. B. N. Martin was read before the Society February 11, 1884, and may be found on page 56 of Volume III. of the Transactions.

Biographical Sketches 85

the Recording Secretary was Samuel T. Carey, the Treasurer was Dr. John C. Jay, and the Librarian and Resident Superintendent was Dr. Asa Gray. Other prominent members were Dr. James E. De Kay, James J. Mapes, Abraham Halsey, Dr. Louis Feuchtwanger, Aaron R. Thomson, Robert H. Brownne, Dr. John Augustine Smith, Dr. William Swift, U. S. N., and Major John Le Conte.

MAJOR DELAFIELD, the President, was an excellent mineralogist, tall and courtly, and with military bearing. He presided with much dignity and to the acceptance of all, and proved a firm and faithful friend to the institution through all its subsequent trials and vicissitudes.

The memory of DR. TORREY'S virtues is too recent to need recalling him to the notice of a passing generation. His amiable, affable and modest demeanor, his kindly smile, his accurate and varied knowledge, won the affections of young and old, even as they continued to do to the end of his useful life. As he was an early friend of my father, my acquaintance with him dated far back, long previous to my connection with the Society.

WILLIAM COOPER was a man of attractive appearance and polished manner, and was a most accomplished zoölogist, as is evinced by his papers in the early volumes of the Annals of the Lyceum. * * * *

Another leading zoölogist of that day was DR. JAMES E. DE KAY. He was a short, square-built, dark-complexioned man, of grave aspect, but very courteous in manner. He entered the Society in 1819, and the early volumes of the Annals are enriched with several valuable papers from his pen. Soon after 1836 he was appointed zoölogist in connection with the New York State Survey upon the Geology and Natural History of the State. Four quarto volumes, beautifully illustrated, embody the results of De Kay's labor. Most of the work upon these volumes was performed in an upper room of the Lyceum building, which he occupied until the building was sold. After the completion of this work he removed to Oyster Bay, Long Island, where he died in 1851.

DR. VAN RENSSELAER was the author of an elementary work upon geology. He was a very tall, athletic man, and said to be the first American who had reached the summit of Mt. Blanc.

SAMUEL T. CAREY and his brother, John Carey, were merchants in the China trade, and I think of English birth. Both were enthusiastic botanists, and the latter contributed to the early editions of Gray's Manual of Botany the elaboration of the genus Carex. Samuel T. Carey came into the Society in 1831. * * * * John was not a member of the Lyceum.

Another leading botanist of that period was ABRAHAM HALSEY, elected in 1818. In early life he had been the cashier and accountant for the large foundry establishment of James P. Allaire, at Corlear's Hook, and at the time I speak of he was cashier of a bank in New York or Brooklyn. * * * * He was a slight built, nervous man, very precise and finical in his ways, an exact student, who had paid much attention to the lower forms of vegetable life. The first paper printed in the Annals of the Lyceum was contributed by him in 1823, being a Synopsis of the Lichens of the vicinity of New York.

MAJOR JOHN LE CONTE, elected in 1817, was well versed in both zoölogy and botany. In fact, he was a born naturalist, and the variety and excellence of his papers in the Annals testify both to the diversity and thoroughness of his knowledge. At this time he was somewhat of an invalid, and under a manner a little brusque and rough lay a kindly heart; and he was ever ready to extend aid to younger enquirers, who could always find access to the resources of his excellent library. In the Botanical Gazette, Vol. VIII., p. 197, will be found a graceful biographical sketch by Dr. Gray.

DR. ASA GRAY was then, as I have mentioned, the librarian and superintendent of the building, and was twenty-six years of age, a native of Sanquoit, Oneida Co., N. Y. He had made the acquaintance of Dr. Torrey about 1831, who was not long in discovering the promise of his future distinction. He had worked with Dr. Torrey in his Herbarium in 1834 and 1835, and in 1834 read his first paper before the Lyceum, a Monograph of the North American Rhynchosporæ, which is still the best help we have for the study of that genus. His bachelor quarters were in the upper story of the building, and there he diligently employed the hours not occupied with other duties, in studies and dissections, the result of which appeared in several elaborate contributions to the Annals. About this time he began to assist Dr. Torrey in the preparation of the Flora of North America—in fact, he then entered upon the labor which for fifty years has occupied him, and which with other work has placed his name foremost in the ranks of American botanists, and rendered it as well known in Europe as in America. In the summer of this year (1836) he was appointed botanist to Wilkes' exploring expedition to the South Pacific, but the long delay in departure and a subsequent call to the chair of Natural History in the University of Michigan led him to resign the position. Yet, after the return of the expedition, many years later, he was employed to work up its botanical results. Dr. Gray's residence in the building and his position as librarian brought him into frequent and pleasant intercourse with the members of the Lyceum, and in this way began my own acquaintance with him. His manner was peculiarly attractive—his deep, hazel eye, his engaging discourse, drew to him the hearts of all; and the few months of intercourse there enjoyed have left a lasting impression on my mind. In 1838 he visited Europe to examine there the Herbaria containing the collections of Michaux, Pursh and others, and soon after his return assumed the position at Cambridge which he still holds. In November last his seventy-fifth birthday was signalized by the presentation, on behalf of 180 botanists of the United States, of a beautiful silver vase with appropriate floral designs.

I must not omit from the botanists of that day the name of ROBERT H. BROWNNE. He was then a young school teacher, with a strong thirst for knowledge, and too modest to let his acquisitions be known. In 1839 he was elected Recording Secretary, which position he held until 1876. Brownne did more, perhaps, than any one man toward keeping alive the insti-

Engraved for the Eclectic by J J Cade, New York.

PROF. ASA GRAY.
(HARVARD UNIVERSITY.)

tution during its days of discouragement. All the details of work fell upon his shoulders, and he accepted his burden cheerfully. His death occurred February 15, 1879. A brief obituary notice of him appeared in the Bulletin of the Torrey Botanical Club, VI., 291.

DR. JOHN C. JAY was a son of Peter A. Jay, an eminent lawyer of New York, and a grandson of Chief Justice John Jay, a distinguished member of the First Continental Congress. As Treasurer of the Lyceum, which he entered in 1832, he took a very active part in the effort to obtain subscriptions for the new building, and bore the principal burden of planning and superintending its construction. He was then a man of twenty-five or thirty, of light complexion, open and pleasing countenance, and somewhat nervous temperament. He was a conchologist, and his collection was for many years the finest and most complete in the country, and is in the possession of the American Museum of Natural History, which also has the costly conchological library which he had brought together. I am greatly indebted to him for his aid in my early conchological studies, to which I turned my attention about this time—my previous predilection—botany—having been interdicted me on account of threatened trouble in my eyesight. Dr. Jay then lived at 22 Bond street, and for many months I was in the habit of spending with him in his library an hour each Monday evening previous to the meeting of the Lyceum. In 1843 he removed to the family residence in Rye, N. Y., where he is still living.

CHARLES CRAMER was a Russian by birth, but spent many years in this country, and entered the Society in

1834. He was devoted to mineralogy, and had a very excellent private collection, especially rich in Siberian minerals. One day, about 1837 or 1838, he received a message from the Czar that he must return to St. Petersburgh, a message with which he was forced to comply to prevent confiscation of property. His minerals were packed away and stored in the cellar of the Lyceum, and when the latter lost its building they were stored in the cellar of the University, where they remained many years—the owner hoping to return to this country. Despairing finally of this, he wrote to have them sent to Russia, and Mr. Brownne and myself exhumed the boxes, rotten with damp, repacked the minerals and shipped them to Mr. Cramer.

JAMES J. MAPES was a man of very wide and general knowledge. He was best known as a chemist and mineralogist, but he had great literary tastes and histrionic talent, and in earlier days wrote dramatic criticisms for the press. He was short, stout, heavy built, even corpulent, and yet he was one of the most agile dancers I have ever seen. He was the father of Mrs. Mary Mapes Dodge. * * * *

DR. JOHN AUGUSTINE SMITH was a member from 1826, very constant in attendance, and in after years was for a long time one of the two Vice-Presidents. He held a very high position in the medical profession, and in society at large. His head was very massive, and it was said that no other man could wear his hat, and it was believed that he was rather proud of the fact.

ISSACHAR COZZENS was an early member of the Lyceum, having been elected in 1822. At the time I entered I think he must have been living out of the city, but afterwards he became a regular attendant; * * * * and after Dr. Gray went away he was put in charge of the building, and for a while, towards the last of our occupancy, I think he occupied one of the stores and sold minerals, fossils and shells. * * * * * * He was quite an old man, with venerable white hair, mixed his v's and w's badly, and I think he must have died poor.

Among the members of the Lyceum at the time I entered I ought not to omit the name of CAPTAIN MATTHEW C. PERRY, U. S. N., afterwards Commodore, who by his firmness and diplomatic skill opened to us an intercourse with Japan. At the period of which I speak he was Commandant of the Brooklyn Navy Yard, and was a very regular attendant upon our meetings, as I think will appear from the minutes. He was in every way a true friend of science, and without pursuing any special branch, he fostered a taste for knowledge among all his associates and subordinates; was mainly instrumental in establishing the Brooklyn Naval Lyceum, and in all his cruises, whether on the coast of Mexico or in the seas of Japan, he was ever ready to aid in obtaining material for scientific research. His history of the U. S. Expedition to Japan, in three volumes, quarto, is a testimonial to his patriotism, his judgment and his zeal.

Such were some of the prominent members of the Institution at the time when it occupied its new building, just half a century ago. I might (did time and space permit) also allude to others whom I afterwards joined in welcoming. Some of these, as

Brevoort, Lawrence, Dinwiddie and Van Nostra[nd]
are veterans, still on the stage of life. One [or]
two who have passed away I cannot refrain fr[om]
mentioning.

One evening, at a meeting of the Lyceum in its H[all]
on Broadway, appeared a bright, ruddy youth of eng[ag]ing and modest manner, who, by way of introducti[on]
brought a box of beautiful and perfect specimens [of]
Pandora trilineata, a pretty bivalve shell dredged [in]
New York harbor. As this shell had rarely been s[een]
except in single and worn valves, the stranger at o[nce]
became of interest to the conchologists present, a[nd]
soon after became a member of the Society, and [his]
zeal and attainments in conchological and mine[ral]ogical study soon gained him the notice and friends[hip]
of the collectors and laborers in these departmen[ts].
CHARLES M. WHEATLEY, for this was his name, aft[er]wards became widely known for his exploitations [of]
the copper mines of Bristol, Conn., and of the mi[nes]
of lead and copper near Phenixville, Pa. The r[are]
and beautiful crystallizations from these mines w[ere]
eagerly sought throughout Europe, in exchange [for]
European rarities, and thus Mr. Wheatley's priv[ate]
collection, which afterwards went to Union Colle[ge]
Schenectady, was one of the finest of that day. [His]
collection of shells, and that of the Mesozoic fossil[s of]
Pennsylvania, were also extensively known. For ma[ny]
years he was Treasurer of the Lyceum, and even af[ter]
his removal to Pennsylvania the Lyceum was glad [to]
retain the prestige of his name, while Mr. Brow[n]
performed the light duties of the office.

DR. BERN W. BUDD associated himself with

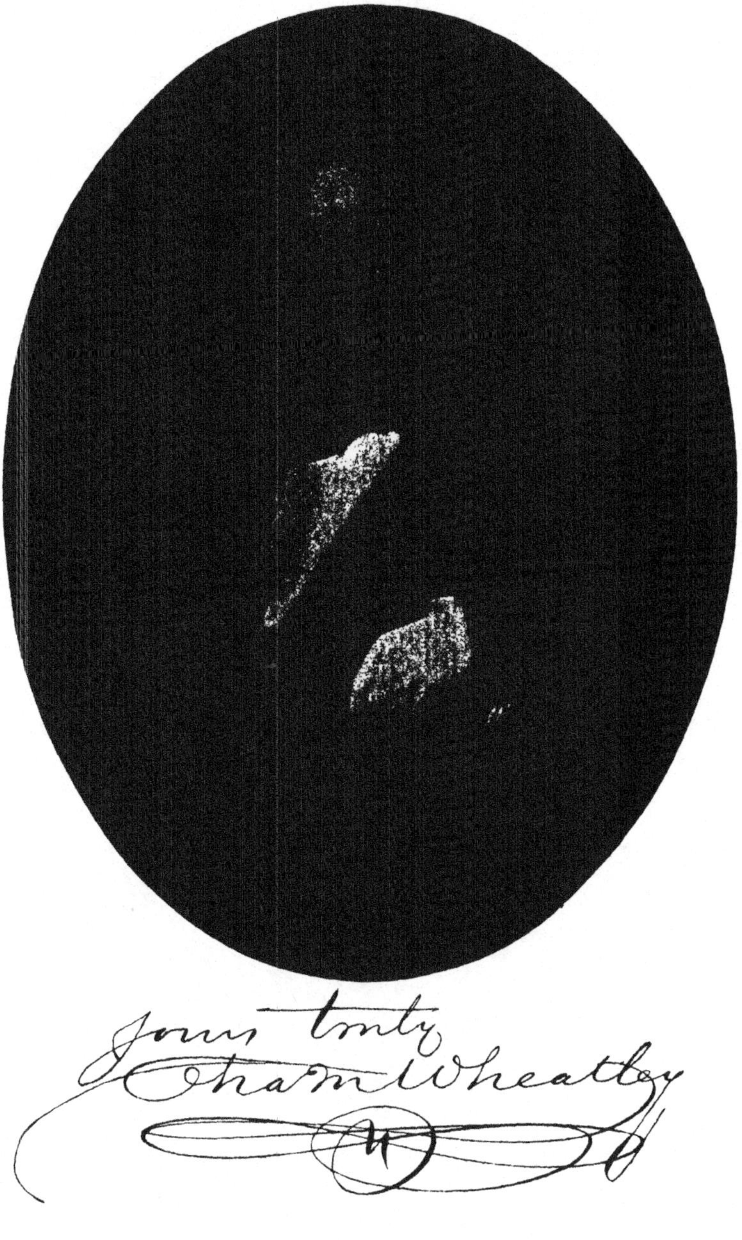
Yours truly
Wm Wheatley

ARTOTYPE, E. BIERSTADT, N. Y

Biographical Sketches 93

Lyceum before the loss of the Broadway building. He had a high standing in his profession, and possessed good judgment and sound common sense. His favorite study was conchology, to which he had been attracted, as he once told me, by the request of his daughter (a deaf mute), that he should tell her something about the classification of some sea shells which he had given her. This daughter afterwards became the wife of Rev. Mr. Gallaudet, an eminent instructor of deaf mutes. De Kay's *Melania gemma* conceals in its specific name a punning reference to Dr. Budd, its discoverer. Dr. Budd was for many years one of the Vice-Presidents of the Society, and was such, I think, at the time of his death. There was in his day a little circle of members of the Lyceum who called themselves the K. K., or Conchological Club, consisting of Dr. Budd, Mr. Wheatley, C. M. Wilber, Charles Congdon and myself.

THOMAS BLAND was of later date, entering the Society in 1852. The Annals of the Lyceum have been enriched by his investigations of the Geographical Distribution of the land shells of the West India Islands. He was a native of England, had spent many years in the West Indies and South America. In Jamaica he had met Professor C. B. Adams, of Amherst College, with whom a warm friendship was formed, and whose favorite line of research was carried out by Mr. Bland after the untimely death of Professor Adams. Of Mr. Bland's suave and pleasing manners, his gentle and self-sacrificing service to all who needed it, I need hardly speak, as he has so recently left us. During many years, as Chairman of the Publication

Committee, he bore the whole burden of the editing of the Annals.*

MR. DANIEL H. BARNES had died several years before my entrance into the Lyceum. But as he was one of the very early members, elected in 1819, and for many years one of its most active and useful men, I ought to mention what I know and remember of him. He was born in 1785, and was an ordained clergyman of the Baptist denomination, though I believe his labors were mostly educational. In 1821 Dr. John Griscom conceived the idea of establishing a school of the higher sort, patterned somewhat after the High School of Edinburgh, in which the monitorial system of instruction should be largely employed. He enlisted the coöperation of some of the leading citizens of New York, and one of his first steps was to secure the aid of a suitable colleague. In a letter written to James Pillaus, then Rector of the High School of Edinburgh, August, 1822, Dr. Griscom says: ' My attention in the choice of a partner was early turned to Daniel H. Barnes, a private teacher of classes in the city. My two younger sons had been for some time pupils in his school. He was an authorized minister or preacher of the Baptist society, but seldom, I believe, exercised the functions of a minister. He was a good Latin and Greek scholar, a tolerably good mathematician, and a good disciplinarian.' †

The school was started in 1824, on the west side of Crosby street, between Grand and Broome streets. I

---

* A memorial notice of Mr. Bland is in Volume V. of the Transactions, page 278.

† Memoirs of Dr. John Griscom, by his son, p. 204.

entered it as a pupil in the autumn of 1826, and remained about three years, and Mr. Barnes was mainly instrumental in fostering and cultivating my taste for natural history. Till then schools had done nothing in this direction; but here, without the use of class books—of which indeed there were none worth the name—and almost without the consciousness of the pupils, a large proportion had their attention directed to the study of nature. Mr. Barnes was, indeed, as Dr. Griscom said, a 'strict disciplinarian,' but I doubt whether any teacher was ever more generally or more deeply revered by his pupils. It was pleasant to see him join in their sports during recess, or to see him surrounded by a group of boys, each with a mineral, a shell, or a plant on which they sought enlightenment from his knowledge. The foundation of my little mineralogical knowledge was laid in a little voluntary class which used to remain after school hours to hear his familiar talks on that subject, illustrated by the specimens of a very good cabinet which he possessed. He was a thorough classical scholar, with a very sensitive ear for rhythm, and nothing was so sure to bring down a stroke of discipline as a false quantity in scanning. Next to this crime he ranked *eating in school*, and no peccadillo that was not absolutely a violation of moral law, was more severely punished.

His scientific work as geologist and zoölogist was highly appreciated in his day. The early volumes of the American Journal of Science and Arts contain most of his papers, and several are found in Vols. I. and II. of the Annals of the Lyceum. One of the objects of a conchological paper which I, long afterwards, contributed to the fourth volume of the Annals was to vindicate the accuracy of Mr. Barnes's conclusions.

Among the pleasant talks and bits of advice given his pupils, I remember one in which he urged the importance of presence of mind in danger, and laid down the rule that no one should ever attempt to jump from a vehicle when the horse was running away. Alas! if he had followed that counsel himself he might have been spared many years longer; but while traveling in a stage coach near Troy, N. Y., the horses took fright, became unmanageable, and he jumped from the coach and was killed, October 27, 1828."

AHTOTYPE. E. BIEHSTADT N. Y.

Thos. Bland

SECTION VI.

Collections.

THIS topic relates mostly to the past. But the cabinets in natural history were so important in the life and work of the Society, and so prominent in the city, that the subject merits more than a passing mention.

Few of the present members of the Society understand that for nearly half a century the collections of the Lyceum filled a place in this city as prominent and as useful for their time as the collections in the American Museum of Natural History do for New York of the present day. This part of the work of the Society certainly had a great educational influence; it stimulated the growth of scientific knowledge in the city and the country at large, and deserved a better public support than it ever received.

The collecting and exhibiting of natural history material was one of the chief objects in the organization of the Lyceum, and up to 1851 the Society nobly fulfilled that purpose. Circumstances have in later years prevented, and probably will ever hereafter prevent, the continuing of that work upon any large scale.

The first record of material donated to the Cabinet is in Bigelow's Magazine, which in the abstract of Lyceum proceedings states that Mr. Rafinesque presented a specimen of the fossil when he read his description of *Tubipora striatula*. This was on March 31, 1817. The Magazine, however, wrongly gives the date as April 9. Upon the latter date Mr. Rafinesque offered a gift of minerals if the Society would pay the Custom House duties. A committee was authorized to procure the minerals and report. At the same meeting " Mr. Rafinesque presented three interesting specimens of granite with schorl, from New Rochelle."

From this time onward the minutes are very largely composed of references to natural history material of all kinds, presented and discussed at the meetings, and destined for the collections, either as donations or to be placed on deposit. The donors were usually presented with the formal thanks of the Society. During the existence of the "lectureship" plan, if the lecturer into whose branch the specimen fell was not able to give a "demonstration" at once, the article was left with him for subsequent report, and when reported upon it was given to the care of the Curators.

After the lectureships were abandoned, the new specimens were reported on by some selected member, or by a special committee.

There is evidence in the early records of great enthusiasm and ability among that small but honored company. Many things are recorded concerning scientific matters which are intensely interesting to us now, and a perusal of the records is a cause sometimes of merriment, often of surprise. The workers of those early years of the century deserve much more credit than we are in the habit of according them. Without the advantages which we possess (advantages which they, indeed, have given us), they accomplished results of which we might to-day be proud. A perusal of the early records of the Lyceum will convince one that many facts and principles for which we take the credit of discovery were not unfamiliar to the scientific students of many years ago. If the proceedings of the Lyceum during its early years were published, simply as they are epitomized in the minutes, they would be invaluable, not merely as a history of the progress of science, but in themselves. Many interesting facts are recorded in the minutes which were never published to the world.

As early as May, 1817, Messrs. Torrey, Rafinesque and Knevels were made a committee to travel, and to explore the natural history and productions of the neighboring counties. They went under the authority of the Lyceum, with credentials from the President. The President and Dr. Townsend, being about to travel, were also sanctioned by the Lyceum.

In June, Drs. Mitchill and Townsend had returned from their exploration of the tract between the Highlands and the Catskill Mountains, and their report, as given in Bigelow's Magazine, is devoted largely to an account of their discovery (May 27–29) of the skeleton of a mastodon near Chester, Orange County. The following extract is in the evident style of Dr. Mitchill:

"Although the fragile and friable nature of these bones might render it impossible ever to connect them into a complete skeleton, the commissioners state it as a matter of the highest probability that, at the aforesaid place, the remains of a mammoth, as huge perhaps as ever walked the earth, reposes in the swamp not more than fifty-four miles from the site of this institution. He has already heard the resuscitating voice of the Lyceum."

Later than this, money was raised by subscription to defray the expenses of an organized effort to obtain a mastodon skeleton for the Museum, which effort was partially successful.

With reference to these explorations Dr. Mitchill wrote :* "The members called it (the Society) the Lyceum, in remembrance of the school founded by that sublime genius, Aristotle, at Athens. Disciples of the 'mighty Stagirite,' they determined, after his example, to be Peripatetics, and to explore and expound the arcana of nature as they 'walked.' * * * * It may be said of this Society, in the words of Virgil, '*Fervet opus redolentque thymo fragrantia mella.*' "

We can imagine that these explorers had many a tale to relate of their thrilling adventures in the swamps of Canal street, the woods of Harlem, and the distant parts of Manhattan Island.

The idea of exploration and of collection of natural history material seems to have been a large element in the purposes and plans of the young Society. Most early notices of the Lyceum mention this part of their

---

* *Medical Repository*, August, 1817.

work. De Kay says, in "Note C," appended to his Anniversary Address, delivered in 1826:

"For some time past a naturalist has been employed in traveling through the country and exploring its various natural productions. One of its members is now in Florida for a similar purpose; and as soon as the state of its funds will admit, it is proposed to employ suitable persons in exploring the region west of the Mississippi." Hardie's "Description of the City of New York," 1828, copies this from De Kay.

Also in "The Picture of New York and Strangers' Guide, &c.," 1828: "Members of this Society are continually employed in exploring expeditions to various parts."

The cabinet grew rapidly from the first. The field for investigation was great and comparatively unexplored. The home field, however, did not satisfy the ambition of the members, and American sailors were urged to bring foreign objects for the New York collection.

Within a few months the Museum of the Society became a recognized institution. Not later than August, 1817, Dr. Mitchill writes:*

"* * * * The Lyceum has already among its articles the *fossil mastodon*, of New York; the *right whale*, of the Atlantic Ocean; the *sword fish*, of Sandy Hook; the new kinds of carp and pike, from the Wall-Kill, and the white wild sheep of the Rocky Mountains, beyond the sources of the Missouri. * * * *

"The Lyceum has taken measures for completing a

---

* *Medical Repository*, August, 1817.

catalogue of the vegetables growing within 100 miles of the city. A committee consisting of C. W. Eddy, M.D., Mr. John Torrey and J. Knevels have made great advances in this important undertaking. The traveling committees of the Lyceum, to the Fishkill and Kaatskill Mountains, and to the adjacent region, have presented reports, observations and discoveries that would honor any society. Among these the papers of C. S. Rafinesque, Esq., merit distinguished approbation. The herbariums are replete with undescribed plants beyond any expectation or belief. * * * *"

The state of the collections ten years after their foundation, and the opinion of the public regarding them, are suggested in the publications of that time.

"Note C" to De Kay's Anniversary Address, 1826, contains the following, which was also copied into Hardie's guide to New York:

"* * * * * * * It has from that period (1818) been steadily, though silently increasing in usefulness and respectability. An extensive cabinet has been formed, which at the present moment contains nearly three thousand mineral species and varieties. No collection in this country is so rich in the department of Herpetology and Ichthyology. It contains more than five hundred species, and must ere long be a place of reference to all who wish to investigate these obscure classes of animals. In addition to the already extensive collections of fossils from various parts of Europe and America, the cabinet contains nearly the entire skeleton of the Mastodon, and large portions of the only North American specimen of the Megatherium hitherto discovered. A new department, that of comparative anatomy, has recently been established, which already contains many valuable preparations, and a series of skulls, nearly two hundred in number, from the different classes of the animal kingdom."

And in "The Picture of New York and Strangers' Guide," page 240, dated 1828, this statement occurs:

"* * * * * The Lyceum has an extensive and choice cabinet of minerals, ichthyology, conchology and organic remains, fossils of Europe, S. America; the skeletons of the Mastodon and Megatherium, and a museum of specimens in comparative anatomy, to all which admission may be readily obtained."

In a historical sketch of the Lyceum printed in the New York *Evening Mail*, April 28, 1868, the Museum is spoken of as follows:

" In 1826 the Museum contained, according to official documents, nearly ' 3,000 mineral species and rarities,' the richest collection of reptiles and fishes in the country—more than 500 species—two hundred skulls, nearly the entire skeleton of the mastodon, and the only known bones at that time o the great sloth, the *megatherium* of North America. Even down to 1843 it was one of the principal museums in the whole country, and contained the types of the original descriptions of multitudes of animals. Its most valuable portions were the minerals, recent fish and echinoderms. As early as 1826 a naturalist had been employed constantly in traveling through the country, and exploring its various natural products. The Herbarium contains several thousand specimens, especially of the plants growing near New York."

In August, 1826, Dr. Mitchill, the former President, and the founder of the Society, presented to the Lyceum his collection of natural history material. A catalogue of this was printed, and copies are still preserved. The collection was very miscellaneous in its character, but much of it had great interest and value. It was arranged upon twelve shelves, and the catalogue contains between four and five hundred numbers. It was claimed that this made the Lyceum's collection of American fossils the most complete in the country at that time.

The Curators' report of 1826 speaks of large additions to the minerals and fishes, and mentions interesting fossils from South America. It also refers to collections of insects, and of vegetable products.

Volume II. of the Annals, 1826–1827, contains a list of donations to the cabinet.

In 1827 at least four rooms were occupied by the Society in the New York Institution. We are left in ignorance as to the size of these rooms, or the space occupied for different purposes.

When the Society was compelled to remove from the New York Institution, the collections were packed in boxes, and a list of these was presented at the meeting, November 29, 1830, and is pasted in the back of the minute-book. It enumerates sixty-two boxes, and other things. Some material was deposited with Mr. Cozzens.

The record of February 22, 1830, states that the Curators were authorized to deposit models of ancient temples with the Historical Society.

In September, 1831, the cabinets were displayed

Yours very truly
John H. Redfield

in the rooms of the Society in the New York Dispensary.

In 1834 the widow of Dr. Mitchill presented to the Lyceum 1,000 mineral specimens; of this collection 400 were displayed, the remainder being duplicates.

A bust of Cuvier and one of Linnæus were received in June, 1835.

At the meeting of October 2, 1837, Dr. James R. Manley presented a table which formerly belonged to the House of Representatives of the Congress of the United States, and formed part of the furniture used by the first Congress, which met in the City Hall. Thanks were returned the donor, and the Librarian was authorized to have an inscribed plate affixed upon it. This table was deposited with the N. Y. Historical Society in November, 1862, and is still there.

Doubtless in the removals of the Lyceum, many other articles have been deposited for safe-keeping with individuals, or with other societies, of which we have no record, and of which all knowledge has passed away.

From 1836 to 1844 the collections were displayed in the Lyceum building (see page 39) in a lofty room with a gallery, which occupied the second and third stories of the front.

When the Society lost its building, the collections were packed and stored for a year in the building of the University. From 1845 to 1851 they were exhibited in the Stuyvesant Institute. But when, in 1851, the University Medical College moved from the latter building to their new building on Fourteenth street, the collections were packed and placed in the cellar of the college. The mounted birds were placed in the museum of the college on the upper floor, and were the only material on exhibition.

During this time, as previously, the material continued rapidly to accumulate. At the weekly meetings a large part of the time was taken in examination and acknowledgment of books and scientific specimens. The latter were packed away in anticipation of a better day, which for the collections was never to dawn. On the fateful night of May 21, 1866, the collections became a thing of memory.

The burning of the cabinets of the Lyceum was an irreparable loss to the world of science. To the Society, however, it was perhaps a blessing in very unpleasant disguise. We can agree with Mr. Redfield, who, as an old member of the Lyceum and one familiar with its cabinet, can more fitly speak. He says: "What I once regarded as a crowning calamity, the destruction of the Museum material, I now regard as a blessing. This may seem paradoxical, but I believe it to be true. The expenses of a scientific society which simply maintains a library and publishes transactions are comparatively moderate, and the work of such a society can be well accomplished in a building of moderate size. But the erection and maintenance of a Museum to contain a full representation of the kingdoms of nature now involves an enormous expenditure and never-ceasing labor, care and anxiety. Happy are those students of nature who can enjoy the benefits of such a Museum without its cost and responsibility."

The Academy still possesses considerable scientific

material, which if displayed might be of much value. But the Society will probably never again undertake the care and support of a large Museum. To the hands of its successor in that work—the American Museum of Natural History—this labor is cheerfully committed; and that young but robust institution can in this work rely upon the sympathy and coöperation of the Academy.

SECTION VII.

Library.

HE books named in the minutes of March 10, 1817, which Dr. Eddy promised to deposit with the Lyceum, are not included in any of the published catalogues of the Library, and if deposited were apparently not presented. The records soon after mention other volumes as being deposited. May 19th the "Purchasing Committee" reported the purchase of two German volumes on Botany for thirty-seven and one-half cents per volume. However, the actual beginning of the Library cannot be determined.

The first printed list of books, which accompanies the Constitution of 1823, bears the date November, 1822, and includes 182 numbers, arranged by authors, alphabetically. A list of donors is appended, the most generous in quantity being J. E. De Kay, who had given thirty-seven numbers, and William Cooper, who had given eighteen.

Originally the Curators had charge of the small Library, and one of their number acted as Librarian. At

ARTOTYPE, E. BIERSTADT, N. Y.

the Annual Meeting of 1824, the office of Librarian was added to the elective offices, and Mr. F. Cozzens was made such officer. He held the office, however, only one year, and was succeeded by James E. De Kay, who was the incumbent for several years. Much of the early growth and firm establishment of the Library are due to his ability, labor and generosity.

At the Annual Meeting in 1826, the close of his first year in the office, De Kay reported 188 additions to the Library, "an increase of as many volumes during the last year as during the whole seven preceding years of our existence as a society." This sudden increase may be partly explained by the fact that in 1825 the Lyceum acquired, as a library fund, the money of the extinct U. S. Military and Philosophical Society, through the good offices of Gen. Swift and other friends who had been members of the defunct organization. This money was in stock of the Eagle Fire Insurance Co., and amounted, with accrued interest, to about $2,500. The following circular letters were printed and distributed, and copies still exist:

To Members of the United States Military and Philosophical Society.

GENTLEMEN,

IT having been suggested by several members of this Society, that for many years past they had ceased to assemble, and that they possessed a considerable fund unappropriated, and therefore totally useless, as it regards the objects for which it was originally intended; and the same gentlemen having expressed a desire to endow the Lyceum of Natural History in New-York with a

Library by means of this fund, we the undersigned, a Committee from the Lyceum, beg leave to address you in its behalf.

The Lyceum of Natural History in New-York was instituted a few years ago, for the purpose of investigating the natural resources and productions of the United States. It is composed of zealous and active members, ardent in the pursuit of science in the several branches of natural history. It has, within a short period, published a complete Flora of the district within fifty miles of the City, and many useful botanical papers have emanated hence. It has also formed a very extensive collection of American vertebrated animals, and perhaps the most general cabinet of American geological specimens, fossil remains, and minerals, in the country. The transactions of the Lyceum are now published in a periodical form at no small expense; and the members look for no other remuneration than what may arise from the consciousness of contributing to the public good. Their exertions, however, have in a great measure been paralysed by the want of those standard European works which are essential to the successful prosecution of their researches. These books, from their nature, are too expensive to be within the reach of an opulent individual, much less of a Society, whose entire resources are devoted to the publication of what it deems useful knowledge.

The undersigned would, therefore, respectfully request, (should you feel inclined to further such pursuits in the manner proposed,) that you would sanction the use of the unappropriated funds of the United States Philosophical Society, for the purchase of a suitable Library for the Lyceum of Natural History in New-York.

We have the honor to be,

Very respectfully,

Your obedient servants,

JOS. DELAFIELD,
J. E. DEKAY,
F. G. KING,
} COMMITTEE.

New-York, May 21, 1824.

New-York, *May* 21, 1824.

SIR,

BELIEVING that the United States Military and Philosophical Society may be considered as dissolved, by reason of a non-compliance with the terms of its constitution for many years past, several of the members have proposed an application of its unappropriated funds to the endowment of the Lyceum of Natural History in New-York with a Library. Since the last meeting of the Military and Philosophical Society, in 1809, deaths and resignations have removed every officer except the Secretaries; and from the provisions of its constitution, requiring annual elections, it is, perhaps at this time, without officers or organization of any kind. Besides which, since the same period, more than one-third of the members have been numbered with the dead. Indeed, the objects for which we had associated have, in part, been anticipated by the liberal patronage of the general Government toward the Military Academy, where an extensive Library is founded; and, in part, by other institutions more local, and consequently more efficient.

There is now belonging to the Military and Philosophical Society a sum exceeding 2000 dollars, deposited in this City. It is sufficient to endow the Lyceum with a useful and lasting memorial of our munificence, by a present of books adapted to its purposes, and I should be pleased if you concur with me in giving your assent to that effect. There is no scientific institution with which I am acquainted, that gives greater promise of utility and honour to the country than the New-York Lyceum. It is conducted with zeal, and is already permanently established and successfully engaged.

Their want of books is a serious drawback to the advancement of these branches of science, and I am not aware that the purposes for which we associated can, under existing circumstances, be more efficiently promoted, nor our remaining funds be more usefully and judiciously employed, than by the adoption of this arrangement.

Should you approve of it, be pleased to signify the same to me by letter. In case the measure is adopted and you would like to become a member of the Lyceum, that Society will, I am assured, be gratified in conferring this, and such other honours as it is in its power to bestow.

I am, respectfully,

Your obedient servant,

J. G. SWIFT,

Last elected Corresponding Secretary.

To
Member of the U. S. Mil. Phil. Soc.

It was found that only 108 members of the dead society were surviving, out of a former membership of 216. Sixty-eight votes were secured in favor of the transfer, the method of which is fully described in the minutes, and the opinions of Chancellor Kent and Counsellor Boyd are there copied in full. Probably this movement had attracted much attention to the Library and stimulated its growth.

The total number of volumes and pamphlets in the Library, as reported by De Kay at this meeting (1826), was 312. Of this number 95 were presented by members, 75 were purchased by the Lyceum, and 142 had been presented by foreigners or by persons not members.

In "Note C," appended by De Kay to his "Anniversary Address on the progress of the Natural Sciences in the United States," delivered before the Lyceum February, 1826, the following relating to the Library occurs : " It now contains about 600 volumes, and the funds of the Military Philosophical Society have been generously presented by the members of that institution for its future increase. The Lyceum is under

pleasing obligation to Col. George Gibbs and Dr. David Hosack of this city, and to B. Dearborn, Esq., of Boston, for many valuable additions to the Library." The passage was copied into Hardie's " Description of the City of New York," 1827.

Mr. J. H. Redfield says, " I remember visiting, when a school-boy, the rooms of the Lyceum in this building (N. Y. Institution) and how I was impressed with wonder at the extent of so large a library devoted to the single subject of natural history."

In 1828 the Library numbered nearly 800 volumes, 240 having been recently added. Volumes I. and II. of the Annals contain catalogues of the books down to December, 1827. The highest number there given is 720. The names of the donors are included.

The following table of additions is given by De Kay in his report of 1829:

1817 to 1825,	291 titles.
1825 to 1826,	189 "
1826 to 1828,	240 "
1828 to 1829,	302 "

The report made in 1830 mentions ninety-two additions.

A classified " Index to the Library " was published in 1830, which makes a pamphlet of seventy-two pages. The highest index number therein given is 1,176, but the number of titles is much greater.

November 18, 1833, the Society being in the New York Dispensary, Dr. G. W. Boyd was made Librarian, and Keeper of the rooms and property, at a small salary. This position he held until 1836. At the meeting, December 9, 1833, he exhibited a visitors' register, which had been ordered November 25, and which is still preserved.

In 1835 De Kay, having retired from the office of Librarian in 1832, evinced his great interest in the Lyceum by presenting it with 249 volumes and 17 pamphlets.

During the first year that the Society occupied its building on Broadway, 1836-7, Asa Gray was the Librarian, and Superintendent of the building. He resigned January 30, 1837, and was succeeded by Robert H. Brownne, who served two years. Issachar Cozzens filled the office from 1839 to 1845, when Mr. Brownne followed, in a second term. A complete list of the Librarians is to be found on pages 55 and 56.

At the removal of the Society from Stuyvesant Institute, in 1851, the Library was placed, through the kindness of the Mercantile Library Association, upon shelves in their gallery. It remained here, in Clinton Hall, until 1867, and so escaped the catastrophe which destroyed the Collections.

For the year ending February 24, 1862, O. W. Morris, who was Librarian for several years, reported an increase of 434 books, the largest increase for one year ever known to that date.

In 1867 the Library is said to have numbered over 3,000 volumes.

From 1867 to 1877 the books were in the Mott Memorial Hall, where the meetings were held. They were arranged in the gallery and were now, for the first time in many years, accessible to the members.

In 1877, chiefly through the efforts of President

Newberry, the Library was transferred to the fire-proof building of the American Museum of Natural History, where it wholly occupied a separate room, and expanded so as to fill several cases in the corridor. Under the arrangement with the Museum, the Academy bore all the expenses of the Library, and expended a large amount of money in cataloguing, binding, care, etc., the Museum simply furnishing shelf-room. Mr. A. Woodward, the Librarian of the Museum, was employed by the Academy to do its work.

The Trustees of Columbia College, in 1884, generously offered to receive the Library on deposit under the same conditions that held at the American Museum—namely, absolute and continued ownership by the Academy, free use of the books by both parties, and the contract to be terminated at the will of either party; and in addition to relieve the Academy of all expenses for care and binding. With the present rapid increase of the Library through exchanges, the yearly cost of binding is a considerable sum, and no money has been expended for that purpose in four years.

Notice of the desire of the Academy to terminate the contract with the Museum was given August 14, 1885; and after negotiation and deliberation extending over some two years the Library was removed to Columbia College during the third week of September, 1886. It is now in the fourth story of the " Library Building" of Columbia College, Madison avenue and Forty-ninth street, and occupies, jointly with the College Herbarium and the botanical books of the College Library, a large, long room, well lighted at both ends, and lighted by electricity on dark days, and until ten o'clock every night of the week except Sunday.

In its new quarters the Library will undoubtedly be of great value to the Society, and to the public. The location is central and easily accessible, and at the meeting place of the Society. The books may be consulted by any person from eight o'clock A. M. to ten o'clock P. M. every day of the year except Sundays, and may be called for from the reading-room on the main floor. At this time no other Library in the city offers equal opportunities to the public. Until such time as the Academy possesses its own building, the arrangement would seem to be such as should be satisfactory to all parties.

Previous to 1876 the books of the Library could, under proper conditions, be removed by the members; losses, however, occurred, some of them irreparable. Since that time the policy has been to regard the Library as one of reference, and no volume can be removed except by special permission of the Council. (See Chap. XII. of By-laws.)

Although the binding is in arrears, the Library is on the whole in excellent condition, and has been since 1877 in constant use, principally by the Curators and workers at the American Museum. Credit is especially due to Prof. Egleston and Dr. Julien as Chairmen of the Library Committee, and to Dr. Elsberg, the late Librarian, for their labors upon the Library during the first years of its stay at the Museum. In later years the cataloguing has been under the direction of Dr. Julien, the present Libra-

rian, and the work of systematizing and keeping the record of accessions has been done by him.

There is no published catalogue of the Library; indeed the growth is so rapid that even the slip catalogue is far behind. The report of Dr. Julien at the Annual Meeting of 1886 shows an increase during the past year of 1,100 numbers, and a total of 8,273 titles.

At the present time the Library is increasing at an unprecedented rate. During the early years of the Society its growth was chiefly from donations by the members and friends, and by purchases. It was the result of the love of science and the sacrifices of the members. But since the Annals have been so widely distributed in all countries, the Library has rapidly grown by exchanges, and now includes sets of the publications of most of the prominent scientific societies of the world. Successful efforts are now making to fill gaps and supply deficiencies.

Considering the size and quality of the Academy's Library; its rapid growth; the advantages which it offers the public in situation, lighting and time, as described above; and its location in the metropolis, it ought to be the most useful scientific library in the United States.

Experts have estimated that it would cost $50,000 to $60,000 to duplicate the Academy's Library, as far as it could be replaced for money.

SECTION VIII.

Publications.

Annals.

HE high reputation, in other countries, of the Society rests upon the "Annals." The first of these octavo volumes was published 1824 to 1826. It contained 410 pages and twenty-nine plates. The following list of contributors includes, it will be seen, the names of many of the most eminent American men of science of that time.

Contributors to Vol. I. of Annals.

Messrs. AUDUBON, BARNES, BIGSBY, DE WITT CLINTON, W. COOPER, F. COZZENS, I. COZZENS, DE KAY, JOSEPH DELAFIELD, R. K. GREVILLE, HALSEY, HARLAN, JAMES, KING, LUDLOW, LE CONTE, MADIANNA, MITCHILL, RENWICK, SAY, SCHOOLCRAFT, SCHWEINITZ, TORREY, TOTTEN, VAN RENSSELAER.

The list of papers is too long to reproduce here, and it would be unnecessary, as the volumes themselves are readily accessible.

At the Annual Meeting in 1826 the Publication Committee made a detailed report, from which we learn that they published an edition of 500 copies, which cost $1,037.16. The subscription price was $4.00, and the receipts from subscriptions was $604.79. There were only forty-seven copies distributed free, as we learn from the report of J. Van Rensselaer, Corresponding Secretary, in 1827. A clause in this report seems to indicate that the English scientific men did not wish to admit that any good thing in science could come out of rebellious young America. The "Corresponding Secretary feels regret at being obliged to announce that the editors of the London scientific periodicals have not noticed our regular and early transmission of the numbers of our Annals in any other manner than by making large extracts from our pages to render their own interesting"; and he then coolly names the disdainful periodicals and editors, the former being well-known journals to-day.

In this case the Society was not without honor at home. "The Picture of New York, etc.," 1828, page 240, in its sketch of the Lyceum, says: "More has been done by this Association towards extending a knowledge of the internal riches of our country, its mineral capacity, its botany and many other branches of science, than by any institution in this city; and this fact is fully evinced by the valuable volumes that have been published by the Society."

At the time of the above writing, Vol. II. of the Annals had been completed, with 480 pages and seven plates, and the following contributors:

Contributors to Vol. II. of Annals.

Messrs. BARNES, BONAPARTE, COOPER, J. F. DANA, DE KAY, LE CONTE, MITCHILL, J. A. SMITH, TORREY.

A circular then issued bore the following heading:

THE ANNALS OF
THE LYCEUM OF NATURAL HISTORY,

CONTINUE TO BE PUBLISHED,

Accompanied with the plates necessary for the illustration of the respective memoirs.

Two volumes, containing thirty-six plates, and nearly 900 pages letter press, are now completed. Price of Vol. I. $4, of Vol. II. $3.50. They may be obtained at the rooms of the Lyceum, or of Messrs. G. & C. Carvill, Broadway.

Up to the time of the change in the name of the Society, 1876, eleven volumes of "Annals" had been published. The third volume of the new series is now complete.

Although these volumes are few in number for the age of the Society, the series is very creditable, of great value, and represents not the gifts of the public or the generosity of the State, but the labors and sacrifices of the members.

The Annals contain descriptions of great numbers of species in various departments of nature, many of them accompanied by figures, and the original specimens being usually placed in the Museum of the Society.

Much additional value is given to the Annals by the number and quality of the illustrations. The total number of plates in the fourteen volumes is two hundred, an average of fourteen plates per volume. Most of these plates, especially the zoölogical ones, are in the best style of art. A few of the zoölogical plates in Vols. IV. and V. are finely colored.

John H. Hinton M.D.

James E. De Kay was the first editor of the Annals, and to him is largely due the reputation which the first two volumes at once gave the Lyceum, at home and abroad. The second part of Vol. II., and Vols. III., VI. and VII. have William Cooper's name first upon the Publication Committee. Vol. V. has W. C. Redfield's name at the head of the list. More recently the late Thomas Bland, and for the last ten years Prof. Daniel S. Martin, have been at the head of the Publication Committee, an office which includes the duties of editorship. It has been the aim of these gentlemen, pursued with great labor and assiduity, to maintain the scientific and literary standing of the Annals at a point not surpassed by any similar publication.

Some of the prominent papers are, upon ornithology, by Audubon, Bonaparte, Baird and Geo. N. Lawrence; upon conchology, by Bland, Binney, Jay, Gulick, Temple Prime, Newcomb and C. B. Adams; upon entomology, by J. L. Le Conte, Grote, Robinson and Packard; upon other branches in zoölogy, by Alexander Agassiz, Gill, Morse and Jordan; upon botany, by Torrey, Gray, De Schweinitz and John Le Conte; upon geology and mineralogy, by De Kay, Delafield, Dana, Newberry, Hitchcock, Julien and Whitfield; upon chemistry, by Leeds and Bolton; upon metallurgy, by Egleston; and upon mechanics, by Thurston. Space will not permit an enumeration of all the eminent names of authors in the Annals, but American science is well represented.

The Annals cannot be said fully to carry out the idea expressed by the name. They contain, as a rule, the more detailed and extensive papers presented to the Society, and are therefore the repository of its most important and permanent work. For the record of the scientific meetings, and for much valuable matter there presented and discussed, another form of publication is necessary.

Proceedings.

Reference will be found in another Section (page 15) to the publication in the first numbers of the American Monthly Magazine of the scientific proceedings of the early meetings of the society. The first printed paper of length is in No. II., Vol. I., of the above named magazine, and was read May 12, 1817, by Dr. P. S. Townsend, entitled, "Observations on Tourmalines, and particularly on those which are found in the U. S." This makes two pages of fine print. The strong leaning of the society, from the very first, towards mineralogy, may be partly explained by the fact that the city lies in a region of crystalline rocks and interesting minerals. May 19th Mr. Pierce showed magnesia from Hoboken, and the topic was understandingly discussed.

This magazine lasted only two years, making four volumes, which contain the earliest record, apart from the minutes, of the scientific proceedings of the Lyceum.

An abstract of the proceedings appeared in 1820 in the second volume of Silliman's Journal, and at intervals in subsequent years. As late as 1844, October 3, the Secretary was authorized to prepare abstracts for publication in the Journal of Arts and Sciences. The Magazine of Useful and Entertaining Knowledge, conducted by N. Sargent and A. Halsey, contained in 1830 abstracts of the proceedings, evidently taken from the minutes. In 1854 abstracts were printed in a newspaper.

The subject of regularly publishing the full scientific proceedings of the Lyceum was frequently considered, but owing to lack of money was never undertaken until 1870. Then it lasted only a year, and failed for want of means, as did a second effort in 1873-4. Some of the chemical proceedings were published in the American Chemist in 1876.

Transactions.

In 1881 another series was begun, with the distinguishing name of "Transactions," and with some irregularity has been continued to the present time. The aim is to print these regularly and promptly during the sessions of the Academy, and to distribute them free to Resident Members and, in exchange for their publications, to prominent American educational institutions, and scientific societies all over the world.

The following are the publications issued to date:

ANNALS (Lyceum of Natural History), Vols. I. to XI.
ANNALS (N. Y. Academy of Sciences), Vols. I., II. and III.
PROCEEDINGS (Lyceum of Natural History), Series I. (300 pp.), Series II. (156 pp.).
TRANSACTIONS (N. Y. Academy of Sciences), Vols. I., II., III. and V. (Vol. IV. not yet issued.)

SECTION IX.

Semi-Centennial Celebration.

UPON the evening of April 29, 1868, in the Great Hall of Cooper Union, there was celebrated the fiftieth anniversary of the acceptance of the charter of the Lyceum, which occurred May 4, 1818.

Plans had been laid to make the occasion one of interest to the public and of help to the Society. Beautifully engraved invitations and tickets were issued in large numbers; fine music was engaged; the newspapers had published favorable notices, and all promised well. But nature's elements were unpropitious. The eminent savants of the Society could wrest from nature her secrets and expose her laws, but they could not at the critical moment control her forces. One of the former members of the society, W. C. Redfield, had immortalized his name by discovering the laws of revolving storms. To avenge this, the heaviest storm of the year was reserved for this special occasion; and, as the President has remarked, the rain poured horizontally.

Very truly yours,
H. Carrington Bolton

The audience was small, judged by the capacity of the hall and the hopes of the active spirits. A few hundred people gathered in spite of the storm. Dr. John Torrey, the only surviving original member, read a "Sketch of the origin and early history of the Lyceum of Natural History," which abounded in reminiscences of early days.* President Barnard of Columbia followed in an address on behalf of science. The title was, "The relation of science to the advancement of civilization, and the expediency of a public provision for the support and encouragement of scientific inquiry."

Rev. Dr. J. P. Thompson was to reply for the city and the people, his subject being, "The elevating influences which scientific organizations exert on great cities." When his opportunity came it was almost eleven o'clock, and denying his power to entertain an audience at that hour, he gracefully declined.

By this time the members were hungry. But their ideas of a fitting feast exceeded those of the originators of the Society, who, at the meeting of organization, according to Dr. Torrey's account given at this anniversary, indulged in only crackers and cheese and a gallon of good beer, for they adjourned to a banquet at the Century Club.

---

* Unfortunately Dr. Torrey did not preserve this paper.

SECTION X.

Change of Name and Constitution.

THE re-naming of the Society was the result of a feeling among the active members that the institution could be made more influential and successful by so extending its scope as not even nominally to exclude any class of scientific workers, and by giving it a name significant of its breadth. The term "Natural History," used in a somewhat general sense at the time of the founding of the Lyceum, had in later years been applied more specifically to biological science.

To make this change in the Constitution, the approval of three-fourths of the resident members was required. This was a difficult thing to obtain, as a large proportion of the membership never regularly attended the meetings. Moreover, there was an active minority opposed to the change. It was accomplished, however, with as little contention and disaffection as could be expected, or is possible, where many people are bound to the existing order.

The reasons and argument for the change were fully

set forth in a report of committee made August 12, 1874, which report was printed and distributed.

Extract from Report of Special Committee
ON THE CHANGE OF NAME OF THE
Lyceum of Natural History in the City of New York.

The Committee report in favor of changing the name of "THE LYCEUM OF NATURAL HISTORY IN THE CITY OF NEW YORK," to "NEW YORK ACADEMY OF SCIENCES," for the following reasons:

First. The present name of the Society is cumbrous from its length.

Second. The term Lyceum has lost its appropriateness for purely scientific organizations, since it has been adopted by theatres, and more especially by circles of spiritualists throughout the country.

Third. The present name of the Society does not accurately express the scope of its deliberations and actions, inasmuch as many of the subjects discussed in its meetings more properly belong to the sciences of Chemistry, Physics, Technology, &c., which are not branches of Natural History.

Fourth. Since our Society is the only purely scientific organization in the city, it should be comprehensive enough in its scope to include in its membership those working in all departments of science, and its catholicity should be expressed by its title, so that no class of scientists should be even nominally, as they now are, excluded from its membership and meetings.

Your Committee is impressed with the conviction that no laudable means should be left untried to secure for this old and honorable institution the position and influence hoped for by its founders, and due to the importance of the position which it occupies in the Metropolitan City of the United States.

As one step toward this end, we earnestly recommend that should assume the broader and higher name of "The New Yor Academy of Sciences."

Respectfully submitted,
J. S. NEWBERRY,
B. N. MARTIN,
H. C. BOLTON.

It is interesting to notice in connection with on point made by this committee—viz., that the nam Lyceum had lost its significance, and was used quit promiscuously—that as far back as in 1835 th Lyceum had to fight to protect its name. In De cember of that year the Society memorialized th Legislature in opposition to the incorporation of an other society with a name likely to be confounde with the "Lyceum of Natural History." It appear that a society of the Fifteenth Ward desired to tak the name of the " New York City Lyceum." On Ma 23d of the following year Dr. Jay informed the meet ing that the Legislature had changed the propose name to the "Stuyvesant Institute."

Another circular, dated November, 1874, was sen to members in order to secure the needed request, i writing, for the change in the Constitution, from one third of the resident membership. This request wa obtained, and May 3, 1875, it was voted to adopt th name " New York Academy of Sciences." The matte was presented to the business meeting in Octobe 1875. At the next business meeting, in November, committee was directed to take steps to secure th approval of three-fourths of the resident members This Committee issued a circular, dated November 15 1875, with which they sent copies of the propose

Yours very sincerely
Albert R. Leeds

Constitution and By-laws, and also the old Constitution and By-laws.

The constitutional three-fourths vote was obtained; and an order from the Supreme Court was issued January 5, 1876, confirming the change, which was accepted by the Society February 21, 1876, when the corporate name of "THE LYCEUM OF NATURAL HISTORY IN THE CITY OF NEW YORK" became "THE NEW YORK ACADEMY OF SCIENCES."

Whatever may be said of the policy of changing the old name, with sixty years of history behind it, there can be no doubt that the present name is one of greater brevity, significance, breadth and dignity.

The radical changes in the laws of the Society were only two in number; but these are of much importance. One change was the creation of a fourth class of members. Under the Lyceum there were Resident, Corresponding and Honorary Members. The Academy includes a fourth class, namely, "Fellows," who are "chosen from among the Resident Members in virtue of scientific attainments or services." It will be seen how the change permits the increase of paying membership by accepting as members persons not professionally scientific, but who are sufficiently interested in science and the Academy to contribute to the cause.

The other change was the concentration of the functions which had previously been scattered through several standing committees into one central committee, denominated the "Council." Nearly all the officers are ex-officio members of the Council. Six members of the Council are annually elected.

There can be no question that this centralization of function and power in one general committee gives greater efficiency and harmony in the Society's work.

The Council has the power of initiating some matters of business, and the consideration of nearly everything. Under the Lyceum one evening each month was mostly occupied in business, and the discussions were sometimes more animated than edifying. Now a few minutes only are necessary to dispose of questions which the Council has considered at length, and another evening is gained for matters scientific.

Included in these two changes of the Constitution there lies a condition, which, though not declared, is yet of exceeding importance as bearing upon the permanence of the character and labors of the Academy. It is required that three of the six elected Councillors, and all of the ex-officio Councillors, except the Treasurer, shall be Fellows. This wise provision guards the scientific character of the Society. It will prevent the alienation of the Academy from the cause of pure science.

The changes made in the By-laws were chiefly those rendered necessary in order to harmonize the By-laws with the Constitution.

But in Chap. VII. of the By-laws another attempt was made to classify the scientific work of the Society. (See pages 10–12, 19.) Four "Sections" were organized, namely: I., Biology; II., Chemistry and Technology; III., Geology and Mineralogy; IV., Physics, Astronomy and Mathematics. To each Section, one evening every month was to be devoted. After a trial of this plan, it was also abandoned. It was found impracticable to change the presiding officer twice during a session, as was necessary if a Section actually conducted the scientific programme for its evening. Moreover, it was impossible so to balance the work as to provide each Section regularly with its proper share of material, or for the Sections to be independently responsible, as was the intention.

During a year, under the present plan, a due variety of matter is presented, but it could not be obtained at set times.

It would seem as if the lesson of experience teaches that the simplest method is the best in the presentation of scientific papers, and that the meetings are most successfully conducted with the least formality.

The changes of name and of organization are evidently justified by their effects upon the Society. There was at once a large increase in paying membership, which has been retained; there was more general interest in the Society, and in science, and the meetings were, and continue to be, more largely attended. There have been a larger number of papers read, more prompt and voluminous publication, and a greater increase in the Library. At every point, excluding the matter of Collections and the Building, the last decade has been the most prosperous in the seventy years of the Society.

SECTION XI.

Membership.

THE several classes of members are defined in Article II. of the Constitution; and some conditions of membership in Chapter I. of the By-Laws. The creation, in 1876, of the class Fellows is described on page 129.

The resident membership of the Society has never been large. One explanation of this circumstance is, probably, to be found in the fact that New York City, being the metropolis and business centre of the country, and absorbed in commercial matters, pure science has received less attention than applied science, and the objects of the Society have never properly interested the people.

Special efforts to increase the number of Resident Members were made in 1867, and in 1876–8, with considerable success. At the present time the number is greater than at any previous period, and an effort is soon to be made to increase the number to one thousand.

The fees and dues of Resident Members were

changed several times in early years. (See page 16.) For a very long period the charges have been Five Dollars; but at the meeting of January 10, 1887, they were raised to Ten Dollars. (See Chapter VIII. of By-Laws.) It is believed that this increase, which places the Academy upon an average with other similar societies, will be helpful in other ways than by increasing its income.

Corresponding members were in the earliest years required to pay dues. At a later time only an initiation fee was exacted, which the proposer of the candidate was expected to pay promptly. (See page 16.) For a great while Corresponding Members have been exempt from any money requirement.

Previous to 1877, only men had been admitted to membership in the Society. But on November 5, 1877, the custom was broken by the election, as Resident Member, of Mrs. Erminnie A. Smith. Since that date several women have been admitted.

Patrons of the Academy.[1]

[Those marked with an asterisk are deceased.]

*Bland, Thomas,
Bolton, Prof. H. Carrington,
Brevoort, J. Carson,
Cotheal, Alex. J.,
*Delafield, Joseph,
Dinwiddie, Robert,
Dodge, William E.,
Egleston, Prof. Thos.,
*Elsberg, L., M.D.,
Field, C. de Peyster,
Greene, J. W., M.D.,
Grinnell, Geo. B.,
Hinton, John H., M.D.,
Lawrence, Geo. N.,
Leeds, Prof. Albert R.,
*Lenox, James,
Livingston, Robert J.,
Newberry, J. S., M.D.,
Prime, Frederick E.,
Prime, Temple,
Sloan, Samuel,
Steward, D. Jackson,
Storrs, Charles,
*Stuart, Robert L.,
*Suckley, Geo., M.D.,
Van Nostrand, H. D.,
*Van Rensselaer, Alex.,
Weston, Henry,
*Wheatley, Charles M.,
Wolfe, Miss Catherine L.

(1) See By-laws, Chapter III., and Chapter VIII., Section 2.

Contributors to the Publication Fund.[1]

[Those marked with an asterisk are deceased.]

Amend, Bernard G.,
American Bank Note Co., A. D. Shepard, Vice-Prest.,
Chamberlain, W. L.,
Coddington, T. B.,
Collingwood, F.,
Crosby, Rev. Howard,
Dodge, Wm. E.,
*Elsberg, L., M.D.,
Herrman, Mrs. H.,
Hildenbrand, W.,
Hoe, Henry,
Julien, Alexis A.,
Krotel, Rev. G. F.,
Lawrence, Geo. N.,
Le Comte, Joseph,
*Lenox, James,
Lord, Franklin B.,
Prime, Temple,
Pyne, Percy R.,
Newberry, J. S., M.D.,
Redfield, John H.,
*Reinhart, B. F.,
Schuyler, Philip,
Stengel, Prof. Fred.,
Steward, D. Jackson,
*Stuart, Robert L.,
Van Beuren, Fred. T.,
Waller, Elwyn,
Weston, Edward W.,
*Wolfe, John D.

(1) See By-laws, Chapter X.

Resident Fellows and Members of the Academy.

(F.) Fellows.
(P.) Patrons.
(S.) Subscribers to Building-Fund.

	ELECTED
Abbott, Frank, M.D.,	1878
Adams, J. W.,	1876
Agnew, C. R., M.D. (F.),	1867
Allen, Prof. J. A.,	1874
Allen, T. F., M.D.,	1876
Amend, B. G. (F.),	1866
Am Ende, Chas. G., M.D.,	1874
Anderson, William G., M.D.,	1886
Arnold, E. S. F., M.D. (F.),	1880
Ashley, Lucius C.,	1886
Atterbury, Rev. Anson P.,	1886
Bailey, James M.,	1868
Barker, Fordyce, M.D. (F.),	1867
Beach, Alfred E.,	1871
Beck, Fanning C. T. (F.),	1868
Bernachi, Charles, M.D.,	1878
Bickmore, Prof. Albert S. (F.),	1873
Banks, David S.,	1886
Bartlett, J. W., M.D.,	1886
Bien, Julius,	1876
Biggs, Charles,	1878
Bjerregaard, Augustin P.,	1886
Blakeman, Birdseye,	1876
Bolles, Hon. Albert S.,	1881

Membership

ELECTED

Bolton, Prof. H. C., Ph.D. (P.) (F.),	1867
Bonnett, Chas. P.,	1885
Bower, William,	1870
Braman, Prof. Benjamin (F.),	1881
Brevoort, J. Carson, LL.D. (P.),	1840
Britton, N. L., Ph.D. (F.),	1880
Bronson, Willett,	1877
Brownell, Silas B. (F.),	1869
Brown, John Crosby,	1867
Brownne, John S.,	1886
Bull, Charles S., M.D. (F.),	1876
Caffall, Robert M.,	1886
Cary, Albert A.,	1886
Caswell, John H. (F.),	1869
Chamberlin, B. B. (F.),	1875
Chandler, Prof. Chas. F. (F.),	1865
Chittenden, L. E. (F.),	1874
Christern, F. W.,	1876
Churchill, A. D. (F.),	1882
Clark, Alonzo, M.D. (F.),	1832
Close, S. L., M.D.,	1877
Colby, Chas. E.,	1883
Collingwood, Francis (F.),	1871
Conklin, W. A.,	1869
Conkling, Alfred R.,	1876
Cooper, Hon. Edward,	1867
Cotheal, Alexander J. (P.) (F.),	1847
Cox, C. F.,	1876
Croly, Mrs. J. C.,	1878
Crooke, John J. (F.),	1867
Crosby, Rev. Howard,	1878

New York Academy of Sciences

ELECTED

Da Costa, Rev. B. F.,	1882
Daly, Hon. Charles P. (F.),	1868
Dana, Wm. S., Lt. Cr., U.S.N.,	1877
Davies, William G.,	1876
Dawson, Benj. F., M.D.,	1876
Day, Austin G.,	1878
Day, Prof. E. H. (F.),	1868
Dederick, E. H.,	1877
Denison, Chas. H.,	1882
Devoe, Fred. W.,	1882
Dewitt, Wm. G.,	1884
Dickerson, Edward N. (F.),	1879
Dickinson, Henri D.,	1881
Diehl, Mrs. Anna Randall,	1880
Dinwiddie, Robert (P.) (F.),	1846
Dittenhoefer, A. J.,	1878
Dix, Rev. Morgan,	1877
Dodge, Wm. E.,	1867
Doremus, Chas. A., Ph.D.,	1876
Doremus, Prof. R. O., M.D. (F.),	1867
Douglass, Andrew E.,	1881
Drummond, Isaac W.,	1877
Drummond, James F.,	1872
DuBois, Eugene,	1876
Dudley, Henry (F.),	1884
Dudley, P. H.,	1884
Eames, C. J., M.D.,	1868
Edsall, Burroughs,	1884
Egleston, Prof. Thomas (P.) (F.),	1861
Ellinger, Morris,	1879
Elliot, S. Lowell,	1884

Membership

	ELECTED
Elliott, Arthur H. (F.),	1881
Elseffer, William L., C.E.,	1885
Ewing, Addison L.,	1886
Fairchild, Prof. H. Leroy (F.),	1879
Fargo, James C.,	1878
Field, C. de Peyster (P.),	1869
Fink, Albert,	1879
Fischer, Chas. S., Jr., M.D.,	1881
Fish, Hon. Hamilton (S.),	1864
Friedrich, J. J., M.D.,	1884
Gallaher, Mrs. Julia A.,	1885
Gallatin, Albert R. (F.),	1840
Gibbons, James S.,	1886
Glass, John,	1882
Gouley, J. W. S., M.D.,	1867
Gratacap, L. P.,	1884
Green, Hon. Andrew H.,	1865
Gregory, Geo.,	1882
Grinnell, George B. (P.),	1871
Guernsey, Egbert, M.D.,	1867
Gunning, Thomas B., D.D.S.,	1878
Gurnee, Walter S.,	1876
Habirshaw, W. M. (F.),	1868
Haddon, Alexander, M.D. (F.),	1878
Hale, Albert W.,	1869
Hamilton, Thomas S.,	1878
Hamilton, Rev. S. M.,	1881
Hartt, James C.,	1878
Hascall, Mrs. Virginia K.,	1881

140   New York Academy of Sciences

ELECTED

Hassler, Charles W.,	1876
Haswell, Charles H.,	1876
Heineman, Henry N., M.D.,	1880
Herrman, Mrs. Henry (P.),	1881
Hewitt, Hon. Abram S. (F.),	1868
Hidden, William E. (F.),	1875
Hildenbrand, William,	1877
Hildreth, D. M.,	1876
Hinton, John H., M.D. (P.) (F.),	1865
Hitchcock, Miss F. R. M.,	1881
Hitchcock, Hiram,	1881
Holbrook, Levi,	1886
Hoe, Henry,	1878
Holder, Chas. F. (F.),	1881
Holder, J. B., M.D. (F.),	1872
Holland, Thomas,	1878
Hooper, Prof. Franklin W.,	1886
Hoyt, Alfred M.,	1878
Hoyt, Henry (S.),	1833
Hubbard, Prof. O. P., M.D. (F.),	1874
Hubbard, Walter C.,	1876
Humphreys, Rev. F. L.,	1880
Hyde, E. Francis,	1881
Ingersoll, William H.,	1876
Ireland, John B.,	1876
Jackson, Joseph H.,	1867
Jacobi, Abraham, M.D. (F.),	1867
James, D. Willis,	1876
Jay, Hon. John (S.),	1836
Jay, John C., M.D. (S.),	1878

Membership

ELECTED

Johnson, Laurence, M.D. (F.),	1880
Judson, Adoniram B., M.D.,	1876
Julien, Alexis A., Ph.D. (F.),	1867
Kelly, William,	1876
Kemp, James F., Ph.D.,	1885
Ketcham, Mrs. A. C.,	1884
Kimber, Rev. Arthur C.,	1878
King, Prof. Clarence,	1878
Knap, Joseph M.,	1886
Krotel, Rev. G. F.,	1877
Kunz, George F. (F.),	1876
Lamborn, R. H., Ph.D.,	1884
Larremore, Hon. R. L.,	1877
Laudy, Louis H., Ph.D. (F.),	1881
Law, Walter W.,	1886
Lawrence, George N. (P.) (F.),	1845
Lawton, Walter E.,	1879
Lecomte, Joseph,	1878
Lee, J. Lawrence, M.D.,	1868
Leeds, Prof. Albert R. (P.) (F.),	1872
Levison, W. Goold (F.),	1872
Lewis, Charlton T.,	1876
Lewis, W. H., Jr.,	1885
Liautard, A., M.D.,	1869
Lichtenstein, Paul,	1876
Lindley, C. L., M.D.,	1886
Livingston, Robert J. (P.),	1864
Loewenthal, Herman, M.D.,	1877
Lord, Benj., M.D.,	1885
Low, Hon. Seth,	1876

	ELECTED
Mackie, Simon F. (F.),	1869
Maclay, W. W.,	1877
Marble, Manton,	1878
Marquand, Henry G.,	1876
Martin, Prof. Daniel S. (F.),	1868
Martin, Edward W.,	1882
Maynard, Prof. Geo. W.,	1881
McCarty, Edwin R.,	1875
McDonald, John,	1882
McNulty, George W.,	1873
Mead, W. H.,	1882
Merrill, F. J. H., Ph.D.,	1886
Mitchell, Edward,	1876
Mitchell, John Murray,	1886
Moldehnke, Rev. E. F.,	1878
Moore, Gideon E., Ph.D. (F.),	1876
Morse, J. H.,	1881
Mott, Alexander B., M.D.,	1867
Mott, Henry A., Jr., Ph.D.,	1874
Mulchahey, Rev. James,	1878
Munsell, C. E., Ph.D.,	1885
Neftel, J. W. K.,	1881
Neftel, William B., M.D.,	1876
Newberry, Prof. John S., M.D. (P.) (F.),	1852
Newton, H. J.,	1871
Nott, F. J., M.D.,	1878
Otis, Fessenden N., M.D. (F.),	1867
Ottendorfer, Oswald, M.D.,	1878
Parmly, D. D.,	1879

Membership

	ELECTED
Parsons, Wm. Barclay, Jr.,	1881
Peabody, Hon. Chas. A.,	1879
Pearsall, R. F.,	1885
Pellew, Chas. E.,	1883
Perley, Joseph L.,	1878
Phelps, William W.,	1878
Pitkin, Lucius, Ph.D.,	1884
Poggenburg, Justus F.,	1885
Potter, Rt. Rev. Henry C.,	1877
Prime, Frederick (S.),	1832
Prime, F. E. (P.),	1864
Prime, Temple (P.) (F.),	1852
Pyne, Percy R.,	1878
Rees, Prof. John K. (F.)	1882
Rice, Charles, Ph.D.,	1876
Ricketts, Pierre de P., Ph.D. (F.),	1871
Ripley, John H., M.D.,	1884
Roberts, Milton Josiah, M.D.,	1885
Rogers, F. M.,	1877
Rousseau, David,	1882
Rudkin, Wm. H. (F.),	1882
Russell, Wm. H.,	1880
Rutherford, Lewis M.,	1864
Sachs, Julius, Ph.D.,	1885
Salter, Richard P.,	1876
Satterlee, F. Leroy, M.D.,	1864
Satterlee, Livingston,	1859
Schack, Frederick,	1876
Schermerhorn, F. A. (F.),	1867
Schnetter, J., M.D.,	1866

ELECT

Schoeney, L., M.D. (F.), ... 18
Schultz, Carl H., ... 18
Schuyler, Philip, ... 18
Seeley, Charles A. (F.), ... 18
Serrell, Lemuel W., ... 18
Shearer, Rev. G. L., ... 18
Shriver, Walter, ... 18
Sieberg, W. H. J., ... 18
Sloan, Samuel (P.), ... 18
Sloane, T. O'Conor, Ph.D., ... 18
Smith, J. Ward, ... 18
Smith, S. Hanbury, M.D., ... 18
Snow, E. L., ... 18
Spencer, Rev. J. Selden, ... 18
Stengel, Prof. Frederick, ... 18
Stevens, Geo. F., M.D., ... 18
Stevens, Prof. W. Le Conte, ... 18
Stevenson, Prof. J. J., ... 18
Steward, D. Jackson (P.) (F.), ... 18
Storrs, Charles, ...
Strong, Charles E., ... 18
Stuyvesant, Rutherford, ... 18

Talbot, Robt. B., M.D., ... 18
Talbott, E. H., ... 18
Taylor, Charles Fayette, M.D., . . . 18
Taylor, Henry L., M.D., ... 18
Terry, Jas., ... 18
Thurber, George, M.D. (F.), ... 18
Todd, A. J., ... 18
Tousey, Sinclair, ... 18
Tows, C. D., ... 18

Truly Yours
Oliver P. Hubbard.

Membership

	ELECTED
Trotter, Alfred W.,	1875
Trowbridge, Prof. W. P. (F.),	1878
Valentine, Lawson,	1877
Valentini, Philip, Ph.D.,	1882
Van Beuren, Fred. T.,	1880
Van Brunt, Cornelius (F.),	1876
Van Nostrand, H. D. (P.),	1850
Van Schaick, Jenkins,	1877
Van Slyck, Geo. W.,	1878
Vaux, Calvert (F.),	1867
Viele, Gen. Egbert L. (F.),	1873
Voorhis, J. R.,	1878
Wall, John L. (F.),	1879
Waller, Elwyn, Ph.D. (F.),	1871
Ward, Miss Mary G.,	1881
Ward, Wm.,	1880
Warner, Alex.,	1882
Warner, James D.,	1878
Weisse, Fanueil D., M.D. (F.),	1875
Weld, Mrs. Amy T.,	1878
Welch, Uriah,	1879
Wenman, Jas. F.,	1878
Weston, Edward W.,	1877
Weston, Henry (P.),	1865
White, Jas. H.,	1881
White, John S., LL.D.,	1885
White, Charles T.,	1874
White, Philip A.,	1878
Whitehouse, F. Cope,	1884
Whitfield, Prof. R. P. (F.),	1879

	ELECTED
Wiechmann, F. G., Ph.D. (F.),	1882
Wiener, Joseph, M.D.,	1876
Wilber, George M.,	1873
Wood, Isaac F.,	1878
Wood, Wm. H. S.,	1885
Woodman, H. T.,	1885
Wurtz, Prof. Henry (F.),	1869
Yates, Joseph,	1879
Youmans, Wm. J., M.D.,	1877

Honorary Members.

(RESTRICTED TO FIFTY.)

	ELECTED
Åckerman, Prof. R., Stockholm, Sweden,	1876
Baird, Prof. Spencer F., Washington, D. C.,	1864
Bunsen, Prof. Robert, Heidelberg, Baden,	1876
Candolle, Prof. Alph. de, Geneva, Switzerland,	1852
Chevreul, Michel Eugène, Paris, France,	1883
Croll, Prof. James, Edinburgh, Scotland,	1876
Dana, Prof. James D., New Haven, Ct.,	1842
Dawkins, Prof. W. Boyd, Manchester, England,	1876
Dawson, Sir William, Montreal, Canada,	1876
De la Rue, Warren, 73 Portland Place, London, England,	1879
Descloizeaux, Prof. A., Paris, France,	1876
Fizeau, H. L., Paris, France,	1879
Frankland, Prof. E., London, England,	1879
Geikie, Prof. Archibald, London, England,	1876
Geinitz, Prof. Hans Bruno, Dresden, Saxony,	1876
Gray, Prof. Asa, Cambridge, Mass.,	1852
Hall, Prof. James, Albany, N. Y.,	1852
Hartlaub, Dr. Gustav, Bremen, Germany,	1864
Hauer, Prof. Franz von, Vienna, Austria,	1864
Helmholtz, Prof. H., Berlin, Prussia,	1876
Hofmann, Prof. A. W., Berlin, Prussia,	1876
Hooker, Sir Joseph D., London, England,	1879
Huxley, Prof. Th. H., London, England,	1876
Joule, James P., Manchester, England,	1879

	ELECTED
Kenngott, Prof. Adolph, Zurich, Switzerland,	1864
Kirchhoff, Prof. Gustavus, Berlin, Prussia,	1879
Kokscharow, Prof. Nicholas von, St. Petersburg, Russia,	1879
Lange, Prof. Victor von, Vienna, Austria,	1876
Lockyer, J. Norman, London, England,	1880
Owen, Prof. Richard, British Museum, London, England,	1879
Quatrefages, Prof. J. L. A., Paris, France,	1879
Rawlinson, Sir Henry Cresswicke, London, England,	1882
Richter, Prof. Th., Freiberg, Saxony,	1876
Thomson, Sir William, London, England,	1876
Torell, Prof. Otto, Stockholm, Sweden,	1876
Tunner, Prof. P. Ritter von, Leoben, Austria,	1876
Verreaux, Julius P., Paris, France,	1866
Young, Prof. Charles A., Princeton, N. J.,	1878

Corresponding Members.

	ELECTED
Abbe, Prof. Cleveland, Washington. D. C.	
Abbott, Dr. Chas. C., Trenton, N. J.,	1883
d'Achiardi, Prof. Antonio, University of Pisa, Italy,	1883
Adams, Rev. H. M., Gaboon, Africa,	1854
Agassiz, Alexander, Cambridge, Mass.,	1866
Angas, Geo. French, London, England,	1864
Appleton, Prof. J. H., Providence, R. I.,	1876
Archbald, Andrew, Paris, France,	1852
Austen, Prof. Peter T., New Brunswick, N. J.,	1878
Ayres, W. O., New Haven, Conn.,	1864
Balch, Geo. T., New York, N. Y.,	1876
Ball, Prof. Valentine, Dublin, Ireland,	1885
Barclay, Robert, England,	1830
Bard, John, Tours, France,	1836
Batchelder, John M., Cambridge, Mass.,	1854
Bayle, Prof. E., School of Mines, Paris, France,	1868
Beadle, E. L., M.D., Poughkeepsie, N. Y.,	1835
Bechler, Lieut. W. H., Newport, R. I.,	1880
Bell, J. Graham, Boston, Mass.,	1878
Bell, James H., Sandusky, Ohio,	1836
Bennet, Rev. Cephas, Tavoy, Birmah,	1847
Berthoud, Edw. L., Golden City, Col.,	1867
Bertrand, Prof. Émile, Rue de Tournon, Paris, France,	1883
Binney, W. G., Burlington, N. J.,	1857
Bishop, Nath. H., Lake George, N. Y.,	1869
Bodley, Prof. Rachel L., Philadelphia, Pa.,	1876
Boissier, E., Geneva, Switzerland,	1852
Bolles, Rev. E. C., Salem, Mass.,	1865
Bombicci, Prof. Luigi, University of Bologna, Italy,	1883

150   New York Academy of Sciences

	ELECTED
Boni, Giacomo, Venice, Italy,	1886
Brandegee, Townsend S., Cañon City, Col.,	1874
Branner, Prof. J. C., Indiana University, Bloomington, Ind.,	1884
Brewster, Wm., Cambridge, Mass.,	1874
Brockett, L. P., M.D., Hartford, Conn.,	1847
Brown, Rev. Samuel R., S.T.D., Yokohama, Japan,	1859
Brunet, Dr., Bahia, Brazil,	1867
Brush, Prof. Geo. J., New Haven, Conn.,	1876
Buck, C. Elton, Wilmington, Del.,	1866
Caldwell, Prof. Geo. C., Ithaca, N. Y.,	1876
Carmichael, Prof. H., Brunswick, Me.,	1876
Castelnau, Count, Paris, France,	1839
Chandler, Prof. W. H., Bethlehem, Pa.,	1876
Chapman, A. W., M.D., Apalachicola, Florida,	1836
Chapman, Prof. E. J., Toronto, Canada,	1877
Chester, Prof. A. H., Clinton, N. Y.,	1877
Christy, David, Baltimore, Md.,	1852
Clark, Thomas, Bristol, England,	1827
Clarke, Prof. F. W., Washington, D. C.,	1876
Clay, Joseph A., Philadelphia, Pa.,	1857
Collett, Prof. John, Indianapolis, Ind.,	1880
Comstock, Prof. Theo. B., Cleveland, Ohio,	1877
Cook, Prof. G. H., New Brunswick, N. J.,	1874
Cooke, Prof. Josiah P., Jr., Cambridge, Mass.,	1876
Cooke, Dr. M. C., London, England,	1868
Cooper, Dr. James G., Haywards, Cal.,	1855
Cope, Prof. Edward D., Philadelphia, Pa.,	1876
Cornwall, Prof. H. B., Princeton, N. J.,	1876
Cory, Charles B., Boston, Mass.,	1880
Cox, Kenyon, Anaheim, Cal.,	1880
Crawford, Jos. A., Davenport, Iowa,	1877
Credner, Prof. Hermann, Leipsic, Saxony,	1866
Crosse, H., Paris, France,	1864
Dale, T. Nelson, Toronto, Canada,	1879
Dall, William H., Washington, D. C.,	1870

Membership

	ELECTED
Dana, Prof. Edw. S., New Haven, Conn.,	1885
Deane, Ruthven, Cambridge, Mass.,	1874
Denning, W. H., Fishkill, N. Y.,	1832
Divine, Dr. S. R., Lake Sheldrake, N. Y.,	1867
Doubleday, Edward, Epping, England,	1838
Douglass, Prof. Silas H., Ann Arbor, Mich.,	1876
Dow, John M., Panama,	1869
Drown, Prof. Thomas M., Boston, Mass.,	1876
Dubois, Henry A., M.D., New Haven, Conn.,	1836
Duns, Prof. John, Edinburgh, Scotland,	1868
Eaton, Prof. Daniel C., New Haven, Conn.,	1860
Edwards, Dr. Arthur M., Newark, N. J.,	1873
Elliot, Daniel G., New York City,	1860
Elliot, Henry W., Washington, D. C.,	1876
Elliott, Prof., John B., Sewanee, Tenn.,	1880
Engelhardt, Francis E., Syracuse, N. Y.,	1869
Ernst, Dr. Adolfo, Caracas, Venezuela, S. A.,	1878
Fairbank, Rev. W., East Indies,	1853
Fay, H. F., Columbus, Ohio,	1858
Fisher, Geo. Jackson, M.D., Sing Sing, N. Y.,	1845
Fitch, Alexander, Carlisle, N. Y.,	1845
Fittica, Prof. F., University of Marburg, Germany,	1879
Fletcher, Prof. Lazarus, London, England,	1885
Ford, Prof. Darius R., Elmira, N. Y.,	1874
Ford, Silas W., Schodack Landing, N. Y.,	1873
Fresenius, Prof. C. R., Wiesbaden, Germany,	1879
Fritz-Gaertner, Dr. R., Tegucigalpa, Honduras,	1878
Gadolin, Gen. Alex., St. Petersburg, Russia,	1868
Gaussoin, E., Baltimore, Md.,	1867
Gibbs, Prof. W., Cambridge, Mass.,	1840
Gilbert, G. K., Washington, D. C.,	1870
Gill, Dr. Theodore, Washington, D. C.,	1858
Gilman, Pres. D. C., Baltimore, Md.,	1876
Girard, Charles, Paris, France,	1852

152 New York Academy of Sciences

	ELECTED
Goessman, Prof. C. A., Amherst, Mass.,	1865
Goode, Prof. G. Brown, Washington, D. C.,	1876
Gordon, Dr. Antonio de, Havana, Cuba,	1883
Grattarola, Prof. Giuseppe, Florence, Italy,	1883
Gravenhorst, J. H. Waters, Bonaire, W. I.,	1882
Green, S. F., Jaffna, Ceylon,	1867
Greenleaf, R. C., Boston, Mass.,	1868
Gregg, Dr. W. H., Elmira, N. Y.,	1865
Gregorio, Marchese Antonio di, Palermo, Sicily,	1883
Grierson, T. M. D., Dumfriesshire, Scotland,	1865
Grote, Prof. Aug. R., Buffalo, N. Y.,	1876
Groth, Prof. Paul, University of Strasburg, Germany,	1877
Guppy, R. J. L., Trinidad, W. I.,	1869
Hagen, Dr. Herman A., Cambridge, Mass.,	1874
Hague, James D., New York, N. Y.,	1874
Hamlin, C. E., Waterville, Maine,	1865
Hancock, D., Demerara, W. I.,	1824
Hanley, Sylvanus, London, England,	1864
Hardin, M. B., Lexington, Va.,	1866
Hartman, W. D., M.D., West Chester, Pa.,	1852
Hawkins, B. Waterhouse, London, England,	1868
Hayden, Prof. F. V., Washington, D. C.,	1862
Hayes, S. Dana, Boston, Mass.,	1876
Henry, Charlton F., U.S.A.,	1853
Henwood, W. Jory, Cornwall. England,	1842
Hepburn, J. M., M.D., Japan,	1859
Hesse-Wartegg, Count Ernst von, New York,	1882
Hexamer, Dr. F. M., Newcastle, N. Y.,	1857
Hickock, W. C., Vermont,	1848
Hill, Prof. Henry B., Cambridge, Mass.,	1876
Himes, Prof. Charles F., Carlisle, Pa.,	1876
Hitchcock, Prof. Charles H., Hanover, N. H.,	1867
Horsford, Prof. E. N., Cambridge, Mass.,	1876
Horton, Letas R., Goshen, Orange County, N. Y.,	1864
Howard, Thos. T., Jr., Perth Amboy, N. J.,	1877
Hunt, Dr. T. Sterry, Montreal, Canada,	1867

Membership 153

	ELECTED
Hyatt, Prof. Alpheus, Cambridge, Mass.,	1876
Hyatt, Prof. James, Stanfordville, N. Y.,	1876
Iles, Malvern W., Denver, Col.,	1875
Irving, Prof. Roland D., Madison, Wis.,	1874
James, Major O. C., Rio Janeiro, Brazil,	1867
Jamieson, Rev. J. M., Sabatha, India,	1847
Jannetaz, Prof. A., College Sorbonne, Paris, France,	1883
Jesup, Rev. Henry Griswold, Hanover, N. H.,	1885
Johnson, Prof. Sam'l. W., New Haven, Conn.,	1876
Jordan, Pres. David S., Bloomington, Ind.,	1876
Joy, Prof. Charles A., Munich, Germany,	1878
Judd, Orange, Middletown, Conn.,	1876
Kendrick, Prof. H. L., U.S.M.A., West Point, N. Y.,	1876
King, C. R., M.D., Philadelphia, Pa.,	1838
King, Prof. William, Glenoir, Galway, Ireland,	1884
Kinney, Prof. J. R., Honolulu, Sandwich Islands,	1867
Knowlton, W. J., Boston, Mass.,	1880
Koenig, Prof. Geo. A., Philadelphia, Pa.,	1876
Koschkull, H. von, Tiflis, Caucasus,	1868
Krebs, H. J., Copenhagen, Denmark,	1867
Kurtz, J. D., U.S.A.,	1865
Lacerda, Antonio de, Bahia, Brazil,	1867
Land, Wm. J., Atlanta, Ga.,	1877
Langley, Prof. J. W., Ann Arbor, Mich.,	1876
Lattimore, Prof. S. A., Rochester, N. Y.,	1876
Lauderdale, J. V., M.D., U.S.A.,	1867
Lea, M. Carey, Philadelphia, Pa.,	1876
Le Conte, Prof. John, Berkeley, Cal.,	1876
Le Conte, Prof. Joseph, Berkeley, Cal.,	1876
Leidy, Joseph, M.D., Philadelphia, Pa.,	1848
Le Jolis, Dr. Auguste, Cherbourg, France,	1876
Le Mercier, Dr. F. G., Paris, France,	1869
Lintner, Prof. J. A., Albany, N. Y.,	1872

	ELECTED
Lockwood, Rev. S., Freehold, N. J.,	1865
Lord, Henry B., Ithaca, N. Y.,	1868
Lowe, Edward J., Nottingham, England,	1857
Lupton, Prof. N. T., Nashville, Tenn.,	1876
Macloskie, Prof. George, Princeton, N. J.,	1876
Mallet, Prof. John W., University of Virginia, Va.,	1876
Marcy, Prof. Oliver, N. W. University, Evanston, Ill.,	1871
Marsh, Prof. O. C., New Haven, Conn.,	1867
Mason, Rev. Francis, Tavoy, Burmah,	1844
Matthew, Prof. George F., St. John, N. B.,	1867
Maynard, C. J., Ipswich, Mass.,	1874
McChesney, Prof. J. H., Chicago, Ill.,	1863
McCormick, Richard H., Arizona,	1869
McMurtrie, W. C., M.D., Washington, D. C.,	1876
Mead, Theodore L., New York City,	1874
Meigs, J. A., Philadelphia, Pa.,	1874
Merrick, Prof. J. M., Boston, Mass.,	1876
Merriam, C. Hart, Locust Grove, Lewis County, N. Y.,	1874
Metcalfe, William, London, England,	1842
Michie, Prof. P. S., West Point, N. Y.,	1885
Minot, Dr. Charles S., Boston, Mass.,	1878
Mixter, Prof. Wm. G., New Haven, Conn.,	1876
Moore, Whitby E., Para, Brazil,	1844
Morch, Otto, Copenhagen, Denmark,	1864
Morris, W. W., U.S.A.,	1851
Morse, Prof. Edward S., Salem, Mass.,	1864
Mortimer, Capt. John H., New York,	1875
Nason, Prof. Henry B., Troy, N. Y.,	1876
Nevius, Rev. Reuben D., Baker City, Oregon,	1867
Newcombe, Wesley, M.D., Ithaca, N. Y.,	1853
Newton, Alfred, Cambridge, England.	1866
Nicholls, Dr. H. A. Alford, Dominica, W. I.,	1882
Nicolis, Sig. Cav. Enrico, Verona, Italy,	1884
Niles, Prof. Wm. H., Cambridge, Mass.	1881

Membership

	ELECTED
Nolan, Dr. E. J., Philadelphia, Pa.,	1880
Nordenskjold, Prof. N. A. E., Stockholm, Sweden,	1868
Ober, Frederick A., Beverly, Mass.,	1879
Oothout, Henry, Stamford, Conn.,	1865
Ordway, Prof. John M., New Orleans, La.,	1876
Orton, Prof. Edward, Columbus, Ohio,	1871
Ostensaken, Baron R., St. Petersburg, Russia,	1857
Packard, Prof. A. S., Jr., Providence, R. I.,	1866
Packard, R. L., Washington, D. C.,	1877
Paine, Prof. John A., Tarrytown, N. Y.,	1877
Palmer, F. Temple, Versailles, France,	1836
Parrot, Rev. Dr. J. W., Addison, Steuben County, N. Y.,	1869
Pecchioli, V., Pisa, Italy,	1846
Peck, Thomas M., Grand Rapids, Mich.,	1853
Peckham, Prof. S. F., Akron, Ohio,	1876
Perkins, Prof. Maurice F., Schenectady, N. Y.,	1876
Pfeiffer, Louis, M.D., Cassel, Germany,	1853
Phené, Dr. J. S., London, England,	1882
Pickering, Prof. Ed. C., Cambridge, Mass.,	1876
Piddington, Henry, Calcutta, India,	1846
Pisani, F., 8 Rue Furstenburg, Paris, France,	1883
Poey, Prof. Andreas, Paris, France,	1869
Poey, Prof. Felipe, Havana, Cuba,	1851
Post, Rev. R. P., Honolulu, Sandwich Islands,	1867
Potter, Prof. W. B., Washington University, St. Louis, Mo.,	1871
Prescott, Prof. Albert B., Ann Arbor, Mich.,	1876
Prime, Prof. Frederick, Jr., Easton, Pa.,	1877
Pumpelly, Prof. Raphael, Newport, R. I.,	1868
Purdie, H. A., Boston, Mass.,	1874
Putnam, Prof. F. W., Salem, Mass.,	1860
Pynchon, Prof. Th. R., Hartford, Conn.,	1876
Quesneville, M. le Dr., Paris, France,	1879
Ramsey, J. G., M.D., Tennessee,	1860

New York Academy of Sciences

	ELECTED
Randall, F. A., Warren, Pa.,	1876
Rau, Dr. Charles, Washington, D. C.,	1877
Rawson, Sir Rawson W., London, England,	1867
Read, M. C., Hudson, Ohio,	1876
Redfield, John H., Philadelphia, Pa.,	1836
Remsen, Prof. Ira, Baltimore, Md.,	1876
Ridgway, Robert, Washington, D. C.,	1874
Robertson, J., Atticus, N. Y.,	1864
Robb, Prof. Wm. Lispenard, Hartford, Conn.,	1886
Roemer, Charles F., Berlin, Prussia,	1845
Roemer, Edward, M.D., Cassel, Germany,	1864
Rogers, Dr. Henry R., Dunkirk, N. Y.,	1882
Rogers, Prof. R. E., Philadelphia, Pa.,	1876
Rosa, W. V. V., M.D., Watertown, N. Y.,	1866
Russell, Israel C., Washington, D. C.,	1876
Sadtler, Prof. Samuel, Philadelphia, Pa.,	1876
Salvadori, T., M.D., Turin, Italy,	1866
Saussure, H. de, Geneva, Switzerland,	1856
Schaeffer, Prof. C. A., Ithaca, N. Y.,	1876
Schweitzer, Dr. Paul, University of Mo., Columbia, Mo.,	1867
Sclater, P. L., London, England,	1856
Scudder, Prof. Samuel H., Cambridge, Mass.,	1876
Sherwood, Andrew, Mansfield, Pa.,	1876
Sinclair, William, West Hoboken, N. J.,	1847
Skinner, Ezekiel, M.D., Liberia,	1837
Slosson, Charles, Buffalo, N. Y.,	1885
Smith, Charles E., Philadelphia, Pa.,	1866
Smith, J. Bryant, Kingston, Jamaica, W. I.,	1852
Smith, Sanderson, Staten Island, N. Y.,	1854
Smith, T. L., M.D., U.S.N.,	1849
Sorby, Henry C., Sheffield, England,	1858
Sprang, Norman, Etna, Alleghany County, Pa.,	1876
Stearns, Robert E. C., Berkeley, Cal.,	1876
Stevens, Dr. Richard P., Brooklyn, N. Y.,	1875
Stillman, Charles H., M.D., Plainfield, N. J.,	1840
Stillman, J. B., M.D., Texas,	1855

Membership

ELECTED

Stoebner, Prof. F. W., Westfield, Mass., ... 1882
Storer, Prof. F. H., Jamaica Plains, Mass., ... 1876
Stout, A. A., M.D., U.S.N., ... 1847
Stretch, Richard H., San Francisco, Cal., ... 1865
Stuart, A. P. S., Lincoln, Neb., ... 1876

Taber, Augustus, Westchester County, N. Y., . . . 1854
Tajore, The Maharajah Sowindho Mokun, Calcutta, Hindostan, 1885
Taylor, Alexander S., California, ... 1860
Thomson, James, Paris, France, ... 1845
Thurston, Prof. Robert H., Ithaca, N. Y., ... 1876
Thwing, Rev. E. P., Brooklyn, N. Y., ... 1885
Torrey, H. Gray, Stirling, N. J., ... 1866
Trowbridge, Prof. John, Cambridge, Mass., ... 1877
Tryon, A. W., Philadelphia, Pa., ... 1873
Tryon, G. W., Jr., Philadelphia, Pa., ... 1864
Tuttle, Prof. D. K., Baltimore, Md., ... 1876

Van Heurck, Henri, Antwerp, Belgium, ... 1871
Verrill, Prof. A. E., New Haven, Conn., ... 1867
Villa, Antonio, Milan, Italy, ... 1846
Villa, J. B., Milan, Italy, ... 1846
Vogdes, Lieut. Anthony W., Governor's Island, N. Y., . 1883
Volhard, Prof. Jakob, University of Munich, Germany, . 1879
Vollum, Dr. Edw. P., Jefferson Barracks, Mo., . . . 1880
Voss, Lothair, Berliburg, Prussia, ... 1869

Waldo, Leonard, New Haven, Conn., ... 1876
Walling, Henry F., Boston, Mass., ... 1869
Ward, James W., Buffalo, N. Y., ... 1876
Warren, Rev. Joseph, Allahabad, India, ... 1848
Warring, Prof. Charles B., Poughkeepsie, N. Y., . . 1876
Weissbach, Prof. A., Berg Akademie, Freiberg, Saxony, . 1883
Wheatland, Henry, M.D., Salem, Mass., ... 1858
Wheaton, Dr. J. M., Columbus, Ohio, ... 1875
White, Rev. G. W., Marietta, Ohio, ... 1854
White, Prof. I. C., Morgantown, W. Va., ... 1874

	ELECTED
Winchell, Prof. Alexander, Ann Arbor, Mich.,	1860
Winchell, Prof. N. H., Minneapolis, Minn.,	1878
Wissman, J. F., San Francisco, Cal.,	1869
Wood, Horatio C., M.D., Philadelphia, Pa.,	1866
Woodward, Henry, London, England,	1868
Wormley, Dr. Theodore G., Philadelphia, Pa.,	1874
Worthen, Prof. A. H., Springfield, Ill.,	1867
Wright, Prof. A. A., Oberlin, Ohio,	1874
Wright, Prof. A. W., New Haven, Conn.,	1876
Wynne, James, M.D., Central America,	1857
Yarrow, Dr. H. C., Philadelphia, Pa.,	1876

Subscribers to the Old Building-Fund of the Lyceum.[1]

ALLEN, T.,
ALLEY, SAUL,
ANTHON, JOHN,
ASPINWALL, WM. H.,
AYMAR, J. Q.,
BAILEY, J. J.,
BAKER, CORNELIUS,
BARKER, P. G.,
BARRON, THOMAS,
BEERS, J. D.,
BOORMAN, J.,
BRADHURST, J. M.,
BROWN, JAMES,
BROWN, STEWART,
BRUCE, G.,
BRUEN, G. W.,
CAREY, S. T.,
CARY, HENRY,
CARY, WM. F.,
CLARK, R. S.,
CLARKSON, DAVID,
COCHRAN, RUPERT J.,
COLDEN, D. C.,
COLES, I. U.,
CONSTANT, J. A.,
COOPER, WM.,
COSTER, D. J.,
COSTER, GERARD, H.,
COSTER, JOHN H.,
COSTER, JOHN G.,
COSTER, WASHINGTON,
CRAMER, CHARLES,
CRARY, JOHN S.,
CRARY, PETER,
CURTIS, B.,
DAVIS, CHAS. A.,
DE KAY, JAMES E.,
DE KAY, G. C.,
DELAFIELD, JOSEPH,
DENNING, WM. P.,
DE RHAM, H. C.,
DEVAN, T. T.,
DODGE, JONATHAN,
DORR, G. B.,
DORR, S. F.,
DOUGLASS, GEORGE,
DOUGLASS, WM.,
DOWNER, SAMUEL, JR.,
DUDLEY, H.,
FAILE, E. G.,
FAILE, THOMAS H.,
FEUCHTWANGER, L.,
FIELD, H. W.,
FISH, HAMILTON,
FITCH, ASA,
FLEMING, AUGUSTUS,
FOSTER, ANDREW, Jr.,
FRANCIS, J. W.,
GEBHARD, FREDERICK,
GIBSON, J.,

[1] See pages 37-38, and Chapter II. of By-Laws.

Glover, John,
Goodhue, J.,
Graham, Charles, Jr.
Graves, Edward A.,
Greenfield, J. V.,
Grinnell, Henry,
Grosvener, S.,
Hagarty, James,
Haggerty, John,
Halsey, John C.,
Halsey, Stephen A.,
Hamilton, Al.,
Harmony, Peter,
Harris, Ed.,
Heard, N. T.,
Heckscher, Charles A.,
Heckscher, Ed.,
Hicks, H. W.,
Hicks, J. H.,
Higginson, S.,
Hoffman, L. M.,
Hoffman, Martin,
Hone, J. P.,
Hone, Philip,
Hosack, D.,
How, C. W.,
Howland, G. G.,
Howland, J. H.,
Howland, S. S.,
Hoxie, Joseph,
Hoyt, Henry,
Hull, Oliver,
Hunt, J.,
Jay, Ann,
Jay, John,
Jay, John, Jr.,
Jay, John C.,
Jay, P. A.,
Johnson, Wm.,
Johnston, John,
Jones, D. S.,
Jones, Ed. R.,
Jones, George,
Jones, James J.,
Joseph, J. L.,
Kearny, Philip, Jr.,
Kemble, Wm.,
Kermit, Robert,
Kernochan, Joseph,
King, James G.,
Lawrence, C. W.,
Lawrence, Wm. A.,
Lee, David,
Lenox, James,
Le Roy, Jacob R.,
Lord, Rufus, L.,
Lord, Thomas,
Lorillard, Jacob,
Lorillard, Peter, Jr.,
Low, Cornelius,
Ludlow, T. W.,
Ludlum, Nicholas,
McCracken, H.,
Mackie, J. F.,
March and Benson,
Marshall, J. R.,
Mason, John,
Mauran, O.,
Minturn, R. B.,
Minturn, R. R.,
Morgan, H. P.,
Moore, Wm.,
Moorehead, John,
Morris, Gouverneur,

MOTT, S. F.,
MOULTON, C. F.,
MURRAY, JAMES B.,
MYER, GEORGE,
NORRIE, A.,
OAKLEY, S.,
OGDEN, J. D. P.,
OLMSTED, F. W.,
PACKER, WM. S., Jr.,
PARISH, DANIEL,
PARISH, HENRY,
PAULDING, N.,
PEARSON, J. GREEN,
PELL, F.,
PENFOLD, EDM.,
POST, ALLISON,
POST, J. W.,
PRIME, EDWARD,
PRIME, FREDERICK,
PRIME, RUFUS,
RANKIN, R. G.,
RAY, RICHARD,
RAY, ROBERT,
REMSEN, E.,
REMSEN, PETER,
RICHARDS, GUY,
RHINELANDER, WM. C.,
ROBBINS, G. S.,
ROGERS, GEORGE P.,
RUGGLES, SAMUEL B.,
RUSSELL, ARCH.,
RUSSELL, WM. H.,
ST. JOHN, J. R.,
SANDERSON, E. F.,
SCHENCK, P. H.,
SCHERMERHORN, J.,
SCHERMERHORN, PETER,
SCHIEFFELIN, H. M.,
SCHROEDER, J. F.,
SCHUYLER, ROBERT,
SHELDON, FREDERICK H.,
SHELDON, HENRY,
SMITH, G. G.,
SMITH, J. A.,
SPOFFORD, P.,
STEWART, A. T.,
STOUT, A. G.,
STRONG, JAMES,
STUYVESANT, P. G.,
SUFFERN, THOMAS,
SUTTON, C.,
SWARTWOUT, S.,
SWIFT, WM.,
TAILER, ED. N.,
TALBOT, C. N.,
TAPPAN, ARTHUR,
TILESTON, THOMAS,
TILLOTSON, ROBERT,
THOMPSON, A. R.,
THOMPSON, M. E.,
THROOP, E. T.,
TOMLINSON, WM. A.,
TORREY, JOHN,
VAN RENSSELAER, J.,
VAN RENSSELAER, STEPHEN,
VARICK, A.,
VERPLANCK, SAMUEL,
WADE, E., Jr.,
WAGSTAFF, A.,
WARD, S.,
WETMORE, DAVID W.,
WHITE, WM. A.,
WILCKENS, S. F.,
WILKES, C.,

WILMERDING, W. E.,   WOLFE, CHRISTOPHER,
WOLFE, JOHN D.,   WOODRUFF, J. O.

The following names are in Dr. Jay's account book, but not in any printed list :

COLES, WM. F.,   LEGGETT, SAMUEL,
HOYT, G.,   PRIME, NATHANIEL,
                   REED, LUMAN.

SECTION XII.

Charter, Order of Court, Constitution and By-Laws.

Charter.

AN ACT TO INCORPORATE THE

LYCEUM OF NATURAL HISTORY

IN THE CITY OF NEW YORK.

Passed April 20, 1818.

1. HEREAS, The members of the Lyceum of Natural History have petioned for an act of incorporation, and the Legislature, impressed with the importance of the study of Natural History, as connected with the wants, the comforts, and the happiness of mankind, and conceiving it their duty to encourage all laudable attempts to promote the progress of science in this State—therefore,

Be it enacted by the People of the State of New York, represented in Senate and Assembly, That Samuel L. Mitchill, Casper W. Eddy, Frederick C. Schaeffer, Nathaniel Paulding, William Cooper, Benjamin P. Kissam, John Torrey, William Cumberland, D'Jurco V. Knevels, James Clements, and James Pierce, and such other persons as now are, and may from time to time become members, shall be, and hereby are constituted a body corporate and politic, by the name of LYCEUM OF NATURAL HISTORY IN THE

CITY OF NEW YORK, and that by that name they shall have perpetual succession, and shall be persons capable of suing and being sued, pleading and being impleaded, answering and being answered unto, defending and being defended, in all courts and places whatsoever; and may have a common seal, with power to alter the same from time to time; and shall be capable of purchasing, taking, holding, and enjoying, to them and their successors, any real estate in fee simple or otherwise, and any goods, chattels, and personal estate, and of selling, leasing, or otherwise disposing of the said real or personal estate, or any part thereof, at their will and pleasure: *Provided always*, that the clear annual value or income of such real or personal estate shall not exceed the sum of five thousand dollars: *Provided*, however, that the funds of the said corporation shall be used and appropriated to the promotion of the objects stated in the preamble to this Act, and those only.

2. *And be it further enacted*, That the said Society shall, from time to time, forever hereafter, have power to make, constitute, ordain, and establish such by-laws and regulations as they shall judge proper, for the election of their officers; for prescribing their respective functions, and the mode of discharging the same; for the admission of new members; for the government of the officers and members thereof; for collecting annual contributions from the members towards the funds thereof; for regulating the times and places of meeting of the said Society; for suspending or expelling such members as shall neglect or refuse to comply with the by-laws or regulations, and for the managing or directing the affairs and concerns of the said Society: *Provided* such by-laws and regulations be not repugnant to the Constitution and laws of this State, or of the United States.

3. *And be it further enacted*, That the officers of the said Society shall consist of a President and two Vice-Presidents, a Corresponding Secretary, a Recording Secretary, a Treasurer, and five Curators, and such other officers as the Society may judge necessary; who shall be annually chosen, and who shall continue in office for one year, or until others be elected in their stead; that if the annual election shall not be held at any of the days for that purpose appointed, it shall be lawful to make such election at any other

day; and that five members of the said Society, assembling at the place and time designated for that purpose by any by-law or regulation of the Society, shall constitute a legal meeting thereof.

4. *And be it further enacted,* That Samuel L. Mitchill shall be the President; Casper W. Eddy the First Vice-President; Frederick C. Schaeffer the Second Vice-President; Nathaniel Paulding, Corresponding Secretary; William Cooper, Recording Secretary; Benjamin P. Kissam, Treasurer; and John Torrey, William Cumberland, D'Jurco V. Knevels, James Clements, and James Pierce, Curators; severally to be the first officers of the said corporation, who shall hold their respective offices until the twenty-third day of February next, and until others shall be chosen in their places.

5. *And be it further enacted,* That the present Constitution of the said Association shall, after passing of this Act, continue to be the Constitution thereof; and that no alteration shall be made therein, unless by a vote to that effect of three-fourths of the resident members, and upon the request in writing of one-third of such resident members, and submitted at least one month before any vote shall be taken thereupon.

State of New York, Secretary's Office.

I CERTIFY the preceding to be a true copy of an original Act of the Legislature of this State, on file in this Office.

ARCH'D CAMPBELL,
Dep. Sec'ry.

ALBANY, *April* 29, 1818.

Order of Court.

ORDER OF THE SUPREME COURT OF THE STATE OF NEW YORK

TO CHANGE THE NAME OF

THE LYCEUM OF NATURAL HISTORY IN THE
CITY OF NEW YORK

TO

THE NEW YORK ACADEMY OF SCIENCES.

WHEREAS, in pursuance of the vote and proceedings of this Corporation to change the corporate name thereof from "The Lyceum of Natural History in the City of New York" to "The New York Academy of Sciences," which vote and proceedings appear of record, an application has been made in behalf of said Corporation to the Supreme Court of the State of New York to legalize and authorize such change, according to the statute in such case provided, by Chittenden and Hubbard, acting as the Attorneys of the Corporation, and the said Supreme Court, on the 5th day of January, 1876, made the following order upon such application in the premises, viz.:

> At a Special Term of the Supreme Court of the State of New York held at the Chambers thereof, in the County Court House, in the City of New York, the 5th day of January, 1876:

Present—HON. GEORGE C. BARRETT, *Justice.*

In the matter of the application of the Lyceum of Natural History in the City of New York to authorize it to assume the corporate name of The New York Academy of Sciences.

On reading and filing the petition of the Lyceum of Natural History in the City of New York, duly verified by John S. Newberry, the President and chief officer of said Corporation, to authorize it to assume the corporate name of the New York Academy of Sciences, duly setting forth the grounds of the said application, and on reading and filing the affidavit of Geo. W. Quackenbush, showing that notice of such application had been duly published for six weeks in the State paper, to wit, *The Albany Evening Journal*, and the affidavit of David S. Owen, showing that notice of such application had also been duly published in the proper newspaper of the County of New York, in which County said Corporation has its business office, to wit, in the *Daily Register*, by which it appears to my satisfaction that such notice has been so published, and on reading and filing the affidavits of Robert H. Brownne and J. S. Newberry, thereunto annexed, by which it appears to my satisfaction that the application is made in pursuance of a resolution of the managers of said Corporation to that end named, and there appearing to me to be no reasonable objection to said Corporation so changing its name, as prayed in said petition: Now, on motion of Grosvenor S. Hubbard, of Counsel for Petitioner, it is:

Ordered, That the Lyceum of Natural History in the City of New York be and is hereby authorized to assume the corporate name of The New York Academy of Sciences.

Indorsed: Filed January 5, 1876.

A copy. WM. WALSH, *Clerk*.

Resolution of the ACADEMY, *accepting the order of the Court, passed February 21, 1876.*

And whereas, The order hath been published as therein required, and all the proceedings necessary to carry out the same have been had, Therefore:

Resolved, That the foregoing order be and the same is hereby accepted and adopted by this Corporation, and that in conformity therewith the corporate name thereof, from and after the adoption of the vote and resolution herein above referred to, be and the same is hereby declared to be

THE NEW YORK ACADEMY OF SCIENCES.

Constitution.

ARTICLE I.

This Society shall be styled The New York Academy of Sciences.

ARTICLE II.

It shall consist of four classes of members, namely: resident members, corresponding members, honorary members, and fellows. Resident members shall be such as live in or near the city of New York; corresponding members, such as reside at a distance from said city; and honorary members, such as may be judged worthy, from their attainments in science, to be admitted into the Academy. The number of honorary members shall not exceed fifty. Fellows shall be chosen from among the resident members, in virtue of scientific attainments or services.

ARTICLE III.

All fellows and members shall be elected by ballot. The names of candidates shall be proposed in writing, at least two meetings previous to being balloted for. The affirmative votes of three-fourths of the fellows and members present shall be necessary to elect a candidate; honorary or corresponding members, however, may be elected without previous notice, provided that the ballot on such election is unanimous.

ARTICLE IV.

None but fellows or resident members shall be entitled to vote in the Academy.

Herman LeRoy Fairchild

ARTICLE V.

No fellow or member who shall be in arrears for one year shall be entitled to vote or be eligible to any office in the Academy.

ARTICLE VI.

The officers of the Academy shall consist of a president, a first and a second vice-president, a corresponding secretary, a recording secretary, a treasurer, five curators, and a librarian, who shall be chosen annually on the fourth Monday in February.* The president, vice-presidents and secretaries shall be fellows. There shall also be elected, at the same time, a finance committee of three.

ARTICLE VII.

There shall be elected at the annual meeting six members, at least three of whom shall be fellows, who together with the president, the vice-presidents, the two secretaries, and the treasurer, shall constitute a Council, by whom all business, to be brought before the Academy, shall ordinarily be prepared. Vacancies occurring in the offices or in the Council of the Academy in the interval between the annual elections, may be filled for the unexpired term by special election at any regular business meeting, provided notice of such election shall have been given at a previous regular business meeting.

ARTICLE VIII.

The election of officers and of the Council shall be

---

* See sixth line of Section 3 of the Charter.

by ballot, and the candidates having the greatest number of votes shall be declared duly elected.

ARTICLE IX.

Five members at an ordinary meeting shall form a quorum, and ten at a special or business meeting, a majority of whom, in either case, shall be fellows.

ARTICLE X.

By-laws, for the further regulation of the Society, may from time to time be made.

ARTICLE XI.

* No alteration shall be made in this Constitution, unless by a vote to that effect of three-fourths of the fellows and three-fourths of the resident members entitled to vote under Article V.

---

* This clause must be taken in connection with Section 5 of the Charter, which requires a previous request in writing of one-third of all the resident members (which must be considered in this case as including fellows, as that class of members was not in existence at the time the Charter was granted), submitted one month previous to any vote being taken.

By-Laws.

Chapter I.—*Of Members and Fellows.*

1. No person shall be considered a resident member, until he shall have signed the Constitution and paid his initiation fee; and unless the candidate shall comply with these conditions within six months from the date of his election, such election shall be void. No member in arrears shall be eligible as a fellow.

2. A resident member or fellow removing permanently from the city may, on giving notice thereof, and on payment of his arrears, become a corresponding member; and a corresponding member who removes to the city, with an intention of making it his permanent residence, may become a resident member on complying with the provisions of the first section of this chapter.

3. No person not engaged in the pursuit of some branch of science shall be elected a corresponding member.

Chapter II.—*Of Original Subscriptions.*

1. Every holder (whether original subscriber, transferee or legatee) of a receipt for the sum of one hundred dollars, paid into the treasury of the New York Lyceum of Natural History towards the liquidation of the debt incurred by the erecting of the building formerly the property of the Lyceum, in Broadway, in this city, shall be entitled for himself and his family to free admission to the Museum of the Academy, and to such public lectures as may be delivered on its behalf, which the members have a right to attend. He shall be entitled to the use of the books of the Library; and shall have the privilege of introducing strangers to the Museum and Library, in accordance with the regulations of the Academy.

Chapter III.—*Of Patrons.*

1. Any person may become a patron of the Academy of Sciences by contributing, at one time, one hundred dollars toward the fund for the general purposes of the Society.

2. A patron shall, during his life, be entitled for himself and his immediate family, to the same privileges as an original subscriber.

CHAPTER IV.—*Of Officers.*

1. The President, or, in his absence, one of the Vice-Presidents, or, in their absence, a Chairman *pro tempore*, shall preside at all meetings of the Academy, and shall have a casting vote. He shall preserve order, and shall decide all parliamentary questions, subject to an appeal to the Society. He shall appoint all committees authorized by the Academy, unless otherwise specially ordered.

2. The Corresponding Secretary shall be charged with the correspondence of the Academy. It shall be his duty to be present at all its meetings, to read all communications made to him in his official capacity; to keep a book in which shall be recorded the correspondence of the Academy, and the names of all corresponding members; to lay the same on the table at all regular meetings thereof; to notify corresponding and honorary members of their election; and to report to the Academy on the fourth Monday of February, annually, the state of its correspondence.

3. The Recording Secretary shall be present at all meetings of the Academy, and keep a record of the proceedings thereof. He shall take charge of all papers and documents belonging to the Society; shall keep a corrected list of members and fellows; shall notify all resident members and fellows of their election, and committees of their appointment; and shall give notice to the Treasurer and to the Council of all matters requiring their action.

4. The Treasurer shall have charge of all moneys belonging to the Academy, and, under its orders, of their investment, and shall give good and satisfactory security to the Society for the faithful discharge of the trust, in a sum not less than five thousand dollars. He shall collect initiation fees and annual dues from all members and fellows, all subscriptions made in behalf of the Academy, and any income that may accrue from property belonging to the institution; shall report at the business meeting in January the names of members in arrears; shall give due notice to the Society of the expiration of all policies of insurance that may be effected on its property; and pay all debts against the Society which shall have

been audited by the Committee of Finance, or the discharge of which shall have been ordered by the Academy at a regular business meeting. He shall furnish the Committee of Finance, on due application, with such information of the state of the funds as they may require; and shall report to the Academy, at each business meeting, the condition of its finances, and on the fourth Monday of February, the receipts and expenditures of the entire year.

5. The Librarian shall have immediate supervision and care of the Library, under the general authority of the Library Committee of the Council. All accessions to the Library shall pass through his hands, and he shall enter the titles to the same in a suitable book kept for that purpose. He shall indelibly stamp every book, pamphlet, paper, or other matter, with the stamp of the Society, as prescribed by the Library Committee or Council. He shall periodically make a detailed report of accessions, and on the fourth Monday in February shall make an Annual Report on the condition of the Library.

6. The Curators shall be separately charged with the safe-keeping and arrangement of the several collections, and with the keys of the cabinets. Each Curator shall have his particular department allotted to him when elected. All regulations made by the Curators shall be reported to the Council, and approved of by the Academy, before such regulations shall come into operation.

7. The Curator having charge of any division of the collection, shall alone be authorized to select duplicate specimens from such division for the purpose of exchange or donation; but no exchange or donation shall be made, except such as is authorized by a vote of the Society.

8. The increase and improvement of the collections being the inducement to exchange, it shall be the duty of the Curators to report to the Society all such opportunities to exchange as would favor this object.

CHAPTER V.—*Of the Council.*

1. The President, Vice-Presidents, and Secretaries of the Academy, shall hold the same offices in the Council. In the absence of any of them, officers *pro tempore* may be appointed.

2. The Council shall meet at least once a month, within ten days preceding the regular business meeting of the Academy. Minutes shall be kept of its proceedings, which may be called for at any business meeting, upon a vote of the Academy. Matters of a strictly personal nature, however, need not be entered on the minutes of the Council.

3. Five members of the Council, a majority of whom shall be fellows, shall constitute a quorum; but the Council may appoint an Executive Committee, or business may be transacted at a regularly called meeting of the Council at which less than a quorum is present, subject to the written approval of a majority of the Council, subsequently given to the Secretary, and recorded by him with the minutes.

4. The Council shall prepare all business referred to it by the Academy, and may present any other business at its discretion. It shall frame its own rules and regulations, and determine the time and place of its meetings.

5. The Council shall organize within itself a Committee on Nominations, a Committee on Publication, and a Committee on the Library, to whom, in the intervals of the meetings of the Council, all matters pertaining to these several subjects shall be referred. Their action shall always be subject to the revision of the Council. The names of the persons composing these committees shall be kept publicly posted in the rooms of the Academy.

6. All business prepared by the Council shall be presented to the Academy by the Recording Secretary, or, in his absence, by some other officer of the Council. But the Council may decline to present business at any meeting at which a majority of those present shall not be fellows.

CHAPTER VI.—*Of Committees.*

1. The Committee on Finance shall audit all accounts against the Academy, and shall have the duties and powers of a Committee of Ways and Means. They shall report on financial questions referred to them, whenever called upon to do so by the Academy or the Council.

By-Laws

2. Committees for Special Purposes may be appointed when required.

CHAPTER VII.—*Of Sections.*

1. The Academy shall organize itself into sections, as follows:
    I. Biology.
    II. Chemistry and Technology.
    III. Geology and Mineralogy.
    IV. Physics, Astronomy, and Mathematics.

2. These sections shall be organized with at least a Chairman and a Secretary, and shall be considered responsible for the scientific papers to be presented on the first, second, third and fourth Mondays of each month, respectively. When a fifth Monday occurs it may be devoted to general or special scientific discussions, at the discretion of the Academy or Council. The Academy or the Council may, for sufficient reasons, change or suspend this order.*

CHAPTER VIII.—*Of Initiation Fees, Annual Dues, etc.*

1. Every resident member, at the time of his admission, shall pay into the treasury, as an initiation fee, the sum of ten dollars. All members who become fellows shall pay into the treasury an initiation fee of ten dollars. Resident members and fellows shall be subject to pay an annual fee of ten dollars.†

2. Any resident member or fellow coming under the provision of Chapter II., or who becomes a Patron, shall be exempt from all future annual dues.

3. The Academy may, on account of services, exempt any member or fellow from his annual dues, provided the proposal be made at a regular business meeting, be approved by the Conncil, lie over until the next regular business meeting, and all the members then present agree thereto.

4. If any resident member or fellow, in arrears for his annual dues for over one year, shall neglect or refuse to liquidate the

---

* This method of organization has been suspended, by order of the Academy.

† Corresponding and honorary members are exempt from initiation fees and annual dues.

same within three months after notification by the Treasurer, his name may be erased from the rolls by a two-thirds vote of the members and fellows present at any regular business meeting of the Society; provided that such action shall have been recommended by the Council and at least one month's notice given in writing to the delinquent to show cause why such erasure should not be made.*

5. All contributions received under the provisions of Section 2 of this Chapter, as also those received from the patrons, shall be invested in United States or in New York States securities, and the income derived therefrom be applied to the general purposes of the Academy.

CHAPTER IX.—*Of the Publications.*

1. The publications of the Academy shall consist of the Annals and the Transactions and such other documents as shall be ordered by the Academy.

2. The publications shall be issued under the supervision of the Committee of Publication, and shall be furnished to members, fellows, and subscribers at such rates as may be determined by the Academy.

3. No member or fellow shall publish any part of the proceedings of the Academy, nor any paper read before it, without the consent of the Council, or by a resolution of the Academy.

CHAPTER X.—*Of the Publication Fund.*

1. Contributions may be received towards establishing a Publication Fund; all such contributions shall be invested in United States or in New York State securities, and the income thereof be applied toward defraying the expense of the scientific publications of the Academy.

2. Contributors to this fund in the sum of one hundred dollars or more, at one time, shall be entitled to one copy of all the scientific publications of the Academy appearing subsequently to the date of the payment of their contribution.

---

* See Section 2 of the Charter.

Chapter XI.—*Of the Museum.**

1. All donations shall have the names of the donors affixed thereto.
2. All members shall have access to the Museum, subject to the regulations of the Academy.
3. All deposited specimens shall be labelled with the name of the depositor, and while they remain as such, shall be exclusively under the control of the Academy, and subject to the same uses and regulations as the specimens belonging to it.
4. No person, making a deposit of specimens, shall be allowed to remove them without giving a receipt for the same to the Curator in charge.
5. No specimen contained in the Museum shall be loaned, unless by special permission of the Academy.
6. The Curators shall arrange, in systematic order, all the specimens belonging to the Museum, and keep a catalogue of the same; and shall report, on the fourth Monday in February in each year the state of the property confided to their charge.

Chapter XII.—*Of the Library.*

1. The Library shall be under the control of the Librarian and the Library Committee.
2. No book shall be purchased, or other expense incurred for the Library, except by a recommendation to that effect signed by a majority of the Library Committee, and ratified by the Council.
3. The Library Committee shall designate such books as ought not to be removed† from the rooms of the Academy, which shall be marked on the catalogue, and shall not be taken out without special permission from the Academy.
4. The Librarian shall be furnished with a book, in which he shall keep a regular account of all books borrowed and returned, by inserting the name of the borrower and the book borrowed, the

---

* This chapter has been suspended, on account of the destruction of the Museum by fire.

† By the present rule, no book can be so removed without special permission from the Council.

time when taken out and when returned. In the absence of the Librarian, one of the Library Committee shall keep this record.

5. A volume, not returned within one month, shall incur a fine of fifty cents, and twenty-five cents for each week thereafter.

6. Any injury done to works shall be estimated by the Committee, and the borrower fined accordingly.

7. The Librarian shall report to the Treasurer, from time to time, the fines imposed.

8. No member or fellow shall take out more than two volumes at one time, without special permission from the Council.

9. On the first Monday in June, all books shall be called in and the Library Committee shall examine the Library, and compare it with the catalogue. They shall note all missing books, and report the same, at the next meeting, to the Academy.

CHAPTER XIII.—*Of Meetings.*

1. The ordinary meetings shall be held on Monday evening in each week.

2. The President, or either of the Vice-Presidents, with any five members or fellows, may call a Special Meeting.

3. Special Meetings shall be called by a notice sent to each resident member and fellow, stating the time at which such meeting is to be held, and the object for which it is called.

4. The meeting held on the fourth Monday in February shall be considered a special business meeting.

5. Ordinary meetings shall be held in such place as shall be determined by the Academy or Council. When meetings are not held in the rooms of the Academy it shall be the duty of the Recording Secretary to notify all the fellows and members of the time and place of meeting. All business meetings shall be held in the rooms of the Academy.

6. Visitors at the meetings shall be introduced by one or more members, and their names shall be announced by the President and entered on the minutes.

CHAPTER XIV.—*Of Business.*

1. All business other than such as relates immediately to the

By-Laws 179

cultivation of science, shall be transacted at the first meeting of each month only—except when the Council shall report it as urgent, in which case it may be transacted at any meeting, provided at least a week's notice shall have been given to all members and fellows.

2. The following shall be considered the regular order of business at the ordinary meetings:

    1. The minutes of the preceding ordinary meeting read, and the sense of the members taken thereon.
    2. The names of visitors announced.
    3. Signing of the Constitution by new members.
    4. Announcement of additions to the Library or Cabinets.
    5. Examination of specimens exhibited.
    6. Report of committees not of a business character.
    7. Presentation and discussion of papers previously announced.
    8. Any other scientific business.
    9. Rough minutes read.
    10. Adjournment.

3. The following shall be considered the order of business at the regular business meetings:

    1. The minutes of the preceding business meeting read, and the sense of the members taken thereon.
    2. The names of visitors announced.
    3. Signing of the Constitution by new members.
    4. Announcement of additions to the Library or Cabinets.
    5. Report of the Council.
    6. Reports of Officers.
    7. Reports of Committees.
    8. Deferred business.
    9. New business.
    10. Elections.
    11. Scientific business.
    12. Rough minutes read.
    13. Adjournment.

4. The Rules of Order as set forth in "Cushing's Manual of

Parliamentary Practice," shall be accepted as authoritative in the meetings of the Society.

CHAPTER XV.—*Of Elections.*

1. The Annual Elections shall be conducted as follows:

Nominations may be sent in writing to the Recording Secretary, with the names of the proposers, at any time not less than thirty days before the Annual Meeting; and the Council shall prepare, from the names so proposed, a list which shall constitute the regular ticket. This list shall be furnished to every resident member and fellow at least two weeks before the Annual Election, and be publicly posted during that time in the rooms of the Academy. But any resident member or fellow shall be at liberty to alter this list, or to prepare another.

The ballots shall be received and examined by at least two tellers, appointed by the presiding officer at the Annual Meeting. A list of the persons who have received the greatest number of votes of those present, certified by the tellers, shall then be presented by them to the presiding officer, who shall thereupon declare the said persons elected to their several offices, and shall present the list to the Recording Secretary, who shall enter it on the minutes and file it: the ballot shall be destroyed as soon as the certified list is handed to the presiding officer.

2. Elections for members and fellows shall be held on the first meeting of each month only. Resident members shall be elected as follows: The candidates shall be proposed publicly, in writing, at any meeting, by a fellow or member; and the nominations, together with the name of the person making them, shall be referred to the Council; the report of the Council shall be openly read at the next regular business meeting, upon which the Academy will proceed to a ballot.* Names of candidates for honorary membership shall be presented by the Council.

3. Fellows shall be elected as follows: Candidates shall be recommended to the Council in writing, with the reasons for such recommendation, signed by the proposer; then if the Council see

---

* See Article 3 of the Constitution.

fit, it shall publicly nominate them at a regular business meeting, and the names of such nominees shall be entered on the minutes, and then be posted in some conspicuous place during all meetings held in the rooms of the Academy, at least until the next regular business meeting. They shall be balloted for in the same manner as resident members.

CHAPTER XVI.—*Of General Provisions.*

1. No expenditure shall be incurred on behalf of the Academy, or disbursements made, unless authorized by a vote of a majority of the members and fellows present at a business meeting.

2. Any member or fellow may be censured, suspended, or expelled, for violation of the Constitution or By-Laws, or for any other offense deemed sufficient, by a vote of three-fourths of the members and three-fourths of the fellows present at any regular business meeting; *provided*, that such action shall have been recommended by the Council at a regular business meeting, and one month's notice of such recommendation, and of the offense charged, shall have been given the member accused.

3. No alteration shall be made in these By-Laws, unless such alteration be submitted publicly in writing, at a regular business meeting, be entered on the minutes with the name of the member or fellow proposing the same, and be adopted by two-thirds of the members and two-thirds of the fellows present at a subsequent regular business meeting.

INDEX OF PERSONS.

(Section XI. not included.)

	PAGE
Adams, Prof. C. B	93, 121
Adams, David P	26
Agassiz, Prof. Alexander	121
Akerly, Dr. B. A	22
Akerly, Dr. Samuel	17, 25, 53, 54
Akerly, Samuel	58
Allaire, James P	86
Allen, Prof. John A	56
Allen, ——	21
Amend, Bernard G	56
Ames (painter)	62
Anderson, Dr. Alex	64
Anthon, John	18
Arcularius, Henry	30
Armstrong, John	59
Audubon, John J	72, 118, 121
Aydelott, Dr. B. P	8, 21, 24
Baird, Prof. Spencer F	121
Bang, Hoffman	26
Bard, Dr. Samuel	58
Barnard, Rev. Dr. F. A. P	124
Barnes, Daniel H	30, 52, 53, 54, 75, 94–96, 118, 119
Barrett, Hon. Geo. C	166
Baudoine, Ezekiel R	6, 17, 23
Beck, Dr. John B	5, 6, 7, 23, 54
Beck, Lewis C	6, 25
Beck, Dr. Theod. R	26
Bigelow, H	12, 15, 22, 98
Bigsby, John J	118
Binney, W. G	121
Bland, Thomas	93, 121
Bliss, Dr. ——	4
Bogart, John B	22
Bolton, Prof. H. C	54, 121, 128
Bonaparte, Chas. L	72, 118, 121
Boyd (lawyer)	112
Boyd, George W	55, 113
Boyle (painter)	62

	PAGE
Brevoort, J. C	43, 48, 49, 53, 92
Browere (sculptor)	63
Brown, Robert	17
Brownne, Robert H	55, 56, 73–76, 85, 88, 89, 90, 114, 167
Budd, Dr. B. W	48, 53, 64, 92, 93
Bull, Lucius	55
Campbell, Arch'd	165
Carey, John	75, 86
Carey, Samuel T	54, 55, 75, 85, 86
Carvill (publishers)	120
Casstrom, H	26
Chittenden & Hubbard (attorneys)	166
Clark, Bracey	26
Clark, William H	24
Clements, J	8, 9, 11, 18, 24, 163, 165
Clinton, Gov. De Witt	17, 118
Colden, Hon. C. D	60, 63
Coles, Benj. U	24
Collins, Zaccheus	26
Congdon, Charles	93
Corning, Samuel B	21, 22, 24
Cooper, Dr. Jas. G	73
Cooper, Wm	6, 18, 20, 24, 30, 38, 53, 54, 55, 70–73, 84, 85, 108, 118, 119, 121, 163, 165
Cozzens, Fred. S	30, 55, 109, 118
Cozzens, Issachar	30, 32, 33, 44, 55, 90, 91, 104, 114, 118
Cramer, Charles	44, 89, 90
Cumberland, Wm	18, 25, 163, 165
Cuvier, Baron G	105
Dana, James F	30, 119, 121
Day, Prof. Edward H	56
Dearborn, B	113
De Candolle, Auguste P	17

De Kay, James E............19, 30, 34, 52, 53, 54, 55, 72, 85, 86, 93, 101, 102, 108, 109, 110, 112, 113, 114, 118, 119, 121
Delafield, Dr. Edward......... 67
Delafield, Henry............... 67
Delafield, Maj. Joseph.....30, 31, 33, 34, 38, 42, 45, 48, 49, 51, 52, 53, 64–68, 84, 85, 110, 118, 121
De Schweinitz, Rev. L. D...... 121
Dewitt, Prof. B................ 63
Dinwiddie, Robert.....54, 55, 68, 92
Dodge, Henry................4, 21
Dodge, Henry S................ 25
Dodge, Mrs. Mary Mapes....... 90
Douglass, Capt. ——........... 26
Drake, Jos. Rodman........... 60
Draper, Prof. John W........45, 48
Dudley, P. H.................. 56
Dunlap (painter)............... 62
Durand (engraver)............. 63
Dyckman, Dr. Jacob......21, 22, 24

Ebeling, Prof. ——............ 26
Eddy, Dr. C. W.............3, 4, 5, 6, 8, 9, 11, 12, 13, 18, 21, 23, 52, 102, 108, 163, 165
Eddy, Thomas Jr............6, 24
Edwards, Arthur M............ 56
Egleston, Prof. Thos, 53, 56, 116, 121
Elliott, Stephen................ 26
Elsberg, Louis..............56, 116
Erving, M. D. L. F..........6, 25

Fairchild, Prof. H. L.........55, 56
Fanning, William A............ 26
Feuchtwanger, Dr. Louis....... 85
Field, Hickson W............38, 48
Field, M...................... 33
Forman, George............... 15
Fox, W. W.................... 33
Francis, Henry M.............6, 24
Francis, Dr. John W..........6, 8, 23, 40, 54, 57
Freehauf, Rev. ——........... 26
Fulton, Robert................ 74

Gale, Leonard D..........30, 48, 54
Gallaudet, Rev. Thomas H..... 93
Gibbs, George...........43, 52, 113
Gill, Theodore................. 121
Giraud, Jacob P............44, 55
Graham, Miss ——............ 71
Graves, John J.............30, 54
Gray, Prof. Asa ...55, 75, 85, 86, 87, 88, 91, 114, 121

Greene, Dr. John W........... 49
Greenland, Dr. B. R..........6, 25
Greville, R. K................. 118
Griscom, Dr. John............. 29, 30, 55, 75, 94, 95
Grote, Prof. Augustus R....... 121
Gulick, J. T................... 121

Haines, William A..........49, 53
Halleck, Fitz Greene........29, 61
Halsey, Abraham......52, 53, 54, 75, 85, 86, 118, 122
Hardie, James........101, 102, 113
Harlan, Richard............... 118
Harris, Dr. Thomas............ 26
Heermans, Dr. Corn. P........6, 25
Herring, James................ 63
Hinton, Dr. John H........... 55
Hitchcock, Prof. C. H......... 121
Hodge, James T............... 48
Hoffman, Josiah O............ 64
Homans, Benjamin............ 26
Hosack, Dr. David........61, 113
Howland, ——................ 43
Hoyt, Henry G................ 30
Hubbard, Prof. O. P.........53, 55
Hubbard, Grosvenor S......166, 167
Huntington, Daniel............ 68

Imbert (engraver). 63
Inman, Henry (painter)........ 63
Irving, William S.............. 24
Ives, Dr. A. W................ 2, 3

James (painter)................ 62
James, Edwin.................. 118
Jarvis, John W. (painter)..62, 63, 64
Jay, John..................... 89
Jay, Dr. John C....36, 37, 38, 40, 42, 43, 44, 48, 55, 85, 89, 121
Jay, Peter A................... 89
Jefferson, Thomas............. 17
Jordan, Prof. David S......... 121
Joy, Prof. Charles A......49, 52, 56
Julien, Alexis A......54, 56, 116, 121

Kent (chancellor).............. 112
King, Frederick G.......54, 110, 118
Kissam, Dr. Benj. P...5, 6, 9, 11, 18, 21, 23, 55, 163, 165
Kissam, Dr. D. W............. 21
Knevels, D'Jurco V.....6, 11, 13, 24, 99, 102, 163, 165

Lampdin (painter)............. 63
Latham, Dr. Samuel........... 57

Index of Persons

Lawrence, G. N...49, 53, 56, 92, 121
Lavoisier, Antoine Laurent..... 58
Le Conte, Maj. John....8, 11, 17, 24, 52, 54, 85, 87, 118, 119, 121
Le Conte, J. L................. 121
Leeds, Prof. Albert R....54, 56, 121
Lemoine, Stephen B........... 25
Linnæus, Carl von............. 105
Loomis, Prof. Elias............ 48
Lorillard, P................... 44
Loring, Dr.................... 21
Lossing, Benson J............. 64
Lozier, John.................. 30
Ludlow, Edward G............ 118

MacNevin, Dr. William J...... 26
McDonald, John............... 56
M'Knight, Dr. J. M. S......... 25
Madianna, J. B. Ricord........ 118
Manley, Dr. Jas. R............ 105
Mapes, Jas. J..............85, 90
Marshall, Dr. Henry........... 26
Martin, Prof. B. N....53, 81–84, 128
Martin, Prof. D. S.......53, 56, 121
Martin, John Peter............ 81
Mason, Prof. Cyrus........44, 45, 48
Mathews, Rev. Jas. M.........32, 34
Maxwell, Hugh................ 24
Mayer, Ferd. F................ 56
Meigs, Henry................. 19
Mitchill, Dr. Samuel L...2–8, 11, 13, 15, 16, 18, 19, 23, 27, 30, 52, 57–64, 71, 98–101, 104, 105, 118, 119, 163, 165
Morris, Oran W.............55, 114
Morse, Edward S.............. 121
Morton, Francis..............6, 23
Morton, Henry..............54, 56

Newberry, Prof. John S..52, 53, 115, 121, 124, 128, 167
Newcomb, Dr. Wesley......... 121
Nott, Rev. Eliphalet........... 26
Nuttall, Thomas............... 72

Olmstead, Prof. Denison....... 76, 77, 80, 82
Owen, David S................ 167
Owen, R. B..................6, 25
Owen, B. R. (probable mistake for R. B.).................... 25

Packard, A. S., Jr............. 121
Parisen (painter)............... 63
Parker (painter)............... 63
Paulding, Nath......18, 54, 163, 165

Peale, Rembrandt............, 64
Peixotto, D. L. M..............6, 23
Pell, W. W 42, 43, 44
Perry, Capt. Matth. C......... 91
Pierce, James...18, 24, 122, 163, 165
Pillaus, James................. 94
Platt, Mrs. (sculptor).......... 63
Post, Dr. Alfred C............54, 56
Priestley, Dr. Joseph.......... 58
Prime Temple........49, 55, 56, 121

Quackenbush, Geo. W......... 167

Rafinesque, C. S..4, 10, 11, 12, 21, 22, 26, 98, 99, 102
Redfield, John H......39, 41, 47, 54, 55, 74, 84, 106, 113
Redfield, William C....45, 48, 49, 51, 53, 76, 81, 121, 124
Renwick, James............... 118
Rich, Stephen A............... 8
Roane, Dr. J................6, 25
Robinson, Coleman T.......... 121
Rogers (painter)............... 68

Satterlee, Livingston..........49, 53
Sargent, N.................... 122
Say, Thomas.................. 118
Schaeffer, Rev. F. C..2, 3, 5, 6, 9, 11, 18, 23, 52, 53, 163, 165
Schoolcraft, Henry R.......... 118
Schweinitz, Rev. L. D. de...... 118
Schweitzer, Paul.............. 53
Scoles (engraver).............. 63
Scudder, S. H................. 29
Seely, William A.............. 48
Shepard, Prof. Charles U....... 82
Silliman, Benjamin..........40, 82
Smith, Sir Chas. H............ 26
Smith, Erminnie A............ 133
Smith, James.................. 25
Smith, Dr. J. A..........30, 52, 53, 85, 90, 119
Smith, Dr. J. M............... 21
Smith, William................ 17
Somme, Prof.................. 26
Steinhauer, Rev. Henry........ 26
Stevenson, Dr. J. B............ 21
Stevenson, Prof. J. J........... 56
Steward, D. Jackson 49
Stuart, Robert L..........48, 49, 76
Swift, Gen. J. G..12, 13, 26, 109, 112
Swift, Dr. William............. 85

Taylor, Dr. N. W.............. 82
Thompson, A. R.............38, 85

	PAGE
Thompson, Rev. J. P.	124
Thurber, Dr. George	6
Thurston, Prof. Robert H.	121
Torrey, Dr. John	6, 7, 11, 13, 18, 24, 30, 46, 52, 53, 68–70, 71, 75, 84, 85, 87, 99, 102, 118, 119, 121, 125, 163, 165
Townsend, Chas. C.	6, 25
Townsend, Lewis C.	27
Townsend, Peter S.	2, 3, 4, 8, 11, 19, 21, 24, 54, 99, 122
Townsend, Peter V (probable mistake for P. S. T.)	21
Trott (painter)	63
Trowbridge, Prof. W. P.	54, 56
Van Brunt, Cornelius	56
Van Nostrand, H. D.	49, 92

	PAGE
Van Rensselaer, Jeremiah	30, 36, 54, 84, 86, 118, 119
Wagstaff, Alfred	54
Walsh, William	167
Watkins, Dr. J. S.	16, 21, 22, 25, 27
Weaver (artist)	63
West, Chas. E.	40
Weston, Rev. S. H.	66, 67
Wheatley, C. M.	43, 49, 55, 92, 93
Whitfield, R. P.	121
Wilber, C. M.	93
Williams (painter)	62
Woodward, Anthony	115
Wyman, John W.	25
Yates, Robert	58
Zabriskie, Martin	45

GENERAL INDEX.

(Section XII. not included.)

	PAGE
Academy of Fine Arts	29, 63
Academy of Natural Sc., Phila.	1
	15, 64
Act of Incorporation	19
Addresses, anniversary	18, 19, 40
Age of American Societies	1
Ages of original members	23–27
American Acad. of Arts and Sciences	1
Amer. Assoc. for the Adva. of Science	76, 80
American chemist	123
Amer. Jour. of Arts and Sc.	95, 122
Amer. Monthly Magazine	15
	16, 22, 98, 99, 122
Amer Mus. of Nat. Hist.	49, 50, 89
	97, 107, 115, 116
Amer. Mus. (Scudder's)	29
Amer. Philos. Society	1
Amherst College	69, 93
Annals	48, 71, 87, 93, 94, 95
	96, 118–122, 123
Anniversary Addresses	18, 19, 40
Annual dues	16, 17
Annual meetings	5–7, 18, 20
	28, 109, 117, 118
Astor House	69
Athenæum	66
Attendance at meetings	30, 35
	42, 43, 46, 47, 131
Authors of papers	118, 119, 121
Barclay street	2, 7, 28, 51
Bigelow's Magazine (see Amer. Month. Mag.)	
Biography	57–96
Bond street	47
Boston	1, 17
Botanical Gazette	24, 87
Bristol, Conn.	92

	PAGE
Brooklyn Naval Lyceum	91
Building (see Lyceum).	
Building Committee	34, 36, 38
Building fund	35–39, 48
Building stock	35, 37, 38
Bulletin Torrey Bot. Club	6, 74, 89
Burning of cabinet	50, 106
Business	178, 179
By-Laws	6, 9, 14, 15, 38, 130, 171–181
Cabinet (see Collections).	
Cambridge University	88
Catalogue of Plants, etc.	68
Catskill Mountains	99
Celebration, Semi-Cent.	124, 125
Century Club	125
Certificate of Membership	14
Change of Name	50, 126–131
	166, 167
Charter	6, 7, 18, 19, 38, 124, 163–165
Chester, N. Y.	99
Chicago Academy of Science	72
City Council	29, 30, 31, 32, 61
Classes, of Lyceum	19
"Clermont" (steamboat)	74
Clinton Hall	50, 51
Collections	10, 12, 30, 31, 32, 39
	42, 43, 44, 48, 49, 50, 62
	73, 97–107, 131
College of New Jersey	69
College of Phys. and Surg.	2, 4, 6, 7
	23–27, 28, 46, 59, 63, 66, 68, 69
Columbia College	23–25, 34, 49
	51, 58, 63, 70, 115
Commercial Advertiser	7
Committees	174, 175
on by-laws	6
books	108
building	34, 36, 38
building fund	34, 35

change of name 127, 128
constitution........... 3, 4, 5, 13
exploration............. 99, 102
finance................. 41, 42
flora of New York........... 13
funds of Military Society.... 110
grounds............ 34, 35, 36, 37
lectures................... 9, 10
minerals..................... 98
membership.................. 17
organizations 2, 3
original members........ 8, 9, 21
publications 16, 118, 121
removal of property........ 47
rooms at Stuyvesant Inst... 46
rooms at University........ 45
scientific classes........... 19
specimens.................. 98
subscriptions.......... 19, 44, 45
Common Council... 29, 30, 31, 32, 61
Conchological Club............ 93
Conchology.................. 72, 93
Congress of United States...... 59
Constitution.... 3-8, 13-15, 16, 21, 22
 25, 38, 126-131, 168-170
 adoption of 5, 7
 change of 126-131
 signing of................. 8
Contributors to the Publication
 Fund.................... 135, 176
Contest over Rooms........... 29, 30
"Cooper's Hawk"............. 72
Cooper Union............... 50, 124
Corlear's Hook, New York..... 86
Corporation of City........ 30, 31, 32
Corresp. members.... 9, 16, 25-27, 72
 133, 149-158, 168
Corresp. Secretary.... 6, 8, 17, 18, 54
 119, 165-172
Council 129, 130, 169, 173-174
Councillors of Acad.. 56, 83, 129, 130
Cramer's boxes.............. 44, 90
"Croakers" (poem)........ ... 60
Crosby street school........... 46
Curators... 6, 18, 23, 24, 30, 32, 70, 98
 104, 108, 173
Debt on Library, etc... 42, 44, 45, 48
 on real estate............ 40, 44
Delafield's house 45, 51
Delaplaine's Repository........ 61
Diploma to Pres. Monroe....... 16
Dispensary, N. Y............. 32, 33
Dues, annual.... 16, 17, 132, 133, 175
Duyckinck's Cyclopædia, etc.... 60
Edinburgh High School........ 94

Editors of Annals.............. 121
Elections.............. 168, 169, 180
 of Fellows............ 180, 181
 of Gov. Clinton 17
 of members............. 9, 180
 of officers...... 6, 18, 52-56, 180
Erie Canal 60
Erie Railway.................. 79
Explorations 99, 100, 101, 103
"Fanny" (poem)............ 29, 61
Fellows....... 129, 130, 132, 136, 168
Female High School........... 34
Finances.................... 19, 20
Fire of 1835 13
 of 1866 .... 50, 106
Flora of North Amer.......... 87
 of North. and Middle States.. 69
 71, 75
 of New York............... 13
Franklin street 49
Fund, building........... 35-39, 48
 sustentation 49

Geographical Society......... 50-51
Geological Survey of N. Y.... 69, 86
Glen's Falls, N. Y............ 12
Grand street lot............. 36-37
"Great Moral Picture" (poem).. 61
"Great Western Railway"..... 77
"Great Sea-serpent".......... 17
Greenwich street.............. 49
Guttenberg, N. J............. 72

Hardie's Desc. of N. Y.. 101, 102, 113
Hamilton Hall................ 51
Harlem Railroad............... 79
Harmony Hall............. 5, 8, 28
Hartford & N. H. R. R........ 79
Herbarium 103
Herring's Nat'l Portrait Gal.... 63
Highlands of N. Y............ 99
Historical Soc. of N. Y... 29, 44, 104
Hoboken, N. J................ 72
Honorary members........... 9
 13, 26, 147, 148
Hour of meetings.......... 18, 19
Hudson R. R. R.............. 79

Ichthyology.................. 60
Illustrations of Annals......... 120
Inaugural address............. 8
Income of Lyceum............ 41
Incorporation........ 18, 19, 163-165
Initiation fee....... 16, 132, 133, 175

General Index 189

	PAGE		PAGE
Japan, expedition to	91	Memorial to Corporation	31
Journal of Arts and Sciences	122	Mercantile Library	49, 114
Journal of Commerce	47	Middletown, Conn.	77
		Minute-book	9
Lease of N. Y. Dispensary	33	Minutes of meetings..2–20, 30, 74, 99	
Lectures	9, 10, 11, 40	writing of	7
by Silliman	40	Mortgages	40–45, 48
Lectureship	11, 15, 19, 98	Mosaic cosmogany	40
Legislature of N. Y	58, 59	Mott Memor. Hall	50, 51, 114
charter from	19, 163–165	Mount Holly, N. J	81
memorial to	18		
Letter of Dr. Francis	8	Name of Lyceum	6, 50, 126–129
of Gen. Swift	12		166, 167
Librarian	39, 56, 55, 105	Natural History	9, 10, 11, 19
	109, 113, 114, 169	of New York	86
Library	2, 9, 31, 32, 37, 39, 43, 44	New Jerusalem Church	40
48, 49, 50, 60, 108–117, 131, 177, 178		Newsboys' lodging-house	28
"Library and Athenæum"	34	New Rochelle, N. Y.	98
Library of Delafield	45	N. Y. Academy of Medicine	51
Linnæan classific.	70	"New York City Lyceum"	128
List of members	9, 14, 15, 22, 26	New York College of Pharmacy.	34
Liter. & Philos. Soc	29, 31, 32, 63	" Dispensary	32, 33, 51
Loans to Lyceum	37, 38, 39, 40	" High School	75, 76
London Zoöl. Society	71	" Historical Society	61
Long Island City	64	" Hospital	59
Loss of building	41–44, 50, 93	" Institution	7, 12, 13
Lossing's Mem. on Dr. Anderson	64		28–32, 51
Lyceum, name of	6, 126	" Medical Repository	59
Lyceum building	35, 44, 51, 73	North Hempstead, N. Y	57
	89, 105, 114, 131	Northwestern Dispensary	76
description of	39	Nova Scotia	72
Madison avenue	50	Officers	6, 15, 18, 52–56, 169, 172
Magazine of Amer. Hist	61	"Old almshouse"	29
Magazine of Useful, etc	122	Order of court, etc	166, 167
Manual of Botany (Gray)	86	Organization	5–7, 28
Mayor of N. Y	31	Original members	8, 9, 21–27, 71
Mechanics' Institute	34	Origin of society	2–7, 27, 28
Medical Repository	100, 101	Oyster Bay, N. Y	86
Medical Soc. of N. Y	59		
Meetings	178	Pacific Railroad reports	72
attendance	30, 35, 42, 43, 46	Palæontology	71
	47, 131	Papers in annals	121
first	2–6, 28	" scientific	12, 13, 17, 131
hour of	18, 19	Patrons (of Academy)	134, 171, 175
in Lyceum building	39–44, 51	Philadelphia, Pa	1, 39
of organization	5–7, 28	Phœnixville, Pa	92
places of	28–51	"Picture of New York", etc	101, 119
Members—		Places of meeting	28–51
age of original	27	Popular lecture course	51
corresponding (see corresp. members).		Portraits of Mitchill	62–64
honorary	9, 13, 26, 147, 148, 168	President	6, 8, 18, 19, 23, 27, 30, 31
original	21–27		52, 164, 165
resident (see resident members).		Princeton College	81
Membership	1, 8, 9, 16, 17, 21–27	Proceedings	15, 16, 99, 122, 123
	34, 129, 131, 132–158, 171	Proposals, of members	8

Publication committee....16, 93, 118	Subscriptions to building fund....35
" fund.......135, 176, 177	37, 38, 159-162, 171
Publications.......118-123, 131, 176	Summer vacation............. 30
Purchase of lot...............34-37	Surgeon-General of New York.. 60
Quorum.............35, 42, 43, 170	Tammany Hall............... 49
	"The Shakespeare"............ 28
Ravenswood, N. Y............. 64	Title page of constitution....... 15
Real estate...................34-44	Torrey Botan. Club..6, 69, 70, 74, 89
Recording Secretary.....6, 18, 23, 54	Transactions................. 123
Record of meetings.........2-20, 74	Treasurer.....6, 18, 23, 36, 37, 38, 40
Redfield's house..............49, 51	42, 43, 44, 55, 130, 165
Rental of rooms..............40, 41	169, 172
Resident members.....8, 9, 16, 23-25	Treaty of Ghent.............. 65
27, 72, 123, 129, 132	Trenton Academy............. 81
133, 136-146, 168	Trinity Church............... 66
Resolutions.................... 67	
Revolving storms.............79, 80	Union College................ 92
Rooms......................28-51	U. S. Expedition to Japan...... 91
"Rotunda".................... 31	" Military Academy........ 69
Rutgers Medical College....... 59	" " & Philos. Soc..109-112
Rye, N. Y.................... 89	University of Edinburgh......58, 63
	" " Michigan........ 88
Sale of building.............42-44	" " New York...31, 32, 33
Sanquoit, N. Y................ 87	34, 44, 45, 82, 90, 105
"Savings Bank".............. 32	University Med. College..45-51, 105
Scudder's museum............. 29	
Sections (of Academy)..130, 131, 175	Vacation in summer..........30, 45
Semi-centennial celeb.....7, 124, 125	Vice-President..6, 18, 23, 52, 53, 165
Silliman's Journal...........95, 122	169, 172
Society for promotion, etc...... 58	
Society Library............... 66	Walker street................. 23
Steam Navigation Co........... 78	West Indies................... 93
Stockholders........37, 38, 159-162	Williams College.............. 69
Stores in building............40, 41	
Stuyvesant Inst...45-48, 51, 105, 128	Yale College.............69, 80, 81
St. Matthew's Church.......... 23	
Subscribers to building fund....159-	Zoölogy....................... 8
162, 171	of New York............. 72

BOUND

AUG 31 1943

UNIV. OF MICH.
LIBRARY

3 9015 02327 6895

Q
11
.N538
F3

Fairchild

History of the New York

Academy of Sciences

Printed in Dunstable, United Kingdom